97

RADAR DAYS

Also available in this series:

Radar Days

Wartime memoir of a WAAF RDF Operator

Gwen Arnold

ISIS

LARGE PRINT

Oxford and Orlando

First published in Great Britain 2000
by Woodfield Publishing

Published in Large Print 2002 by ISIS Publishing Ltd,
7 Centremead, Osney Mead, Oxford OX2 0ES
by arrangement with Woodfield Publishing

British Library Cataloguing in Publication Data
Arnold, Gwen
   Radar days. - Large print ed.
   1.Arnold, Gwen 2.Great Britain. Royal Air Force. Women's
   Royal Air Force 3.World War, 1939-1945 - Great Britain -
   Participation, Female 4.World War, 1939-1945 - Personal
   narratives, British 5.World War, 1939-1945 - Great Britain
   - Radar 6.Large type books
   I.Title
   940.5'48141

ISBN 0-7531-9772-3 (hb)
ISBN 0-7531-9773-1 (pb)

Printed and bound by Antony Rowe, Chippenham

FOREWORD

I feel I should explain how this little account came to be written. In the mid-eighties John and I became very interested in family history and spent many days sifting through records at the Public Records Office. Although it was easy to discover when great-great-great grandparents were born, married and died, we were unable to find anything about them as people. What was village life in Dorset like in the early part of the nineteenth century? How did George and Amelia meet? And was the ancestor who stopped increasing his family during the period of the Crimean war in the army and away fighting? There were so many questions we wanted to ask.

All this family history research coincided with the acquisition of a word processor, so I killed two birds with one stone and "played" with our new toy, and at the same time wrote about my childhood and early years. I thought that maybe when my grandchildren became men and women, they perhaps would find the way we lived in the thirties and forties of some interest. I am sure I would have been less forthcoming if I had known that a wider readership would come about, and I blush as I re-read some passages. However, I hope that my story can be considered a small piece of social history — we really were very much influenced by Hollywood, most went to the "pictures" at least once a week, and we were quite Victorian in many ways. I should add that in many places the years mentioned will not "add up". This is because I wrote my little story in the mid-eighties.

Gwen Reading
April 2000

CONTENTS

CHAPTER ONE

"I Was So Happy Then."

For details of our earliest years we depend on images stored in the deepest recesses of the memory, and on the testimonies of our parents. In time we scarcely know where the stories begin and the memories end. In my case, recollections from the age of five or six are very clear; before that time the fusion of images and reported facts cannot easily be disentangled.

Three modicums of information about the day I was born survive. Firstly, my arrival was preceded by a heavy thunderstorm. Perhaps that proved to be something of an inoculation for me, because through the years thunderstorms have never disturbed me. In fact, I rather enjoy storms. Secondly, I made my appearance at 1.30p.m., and lastly, my mother just had time to enjoy a rice pudding before the event!

My mother, in common with most mothers, thought her new baby to be beautiful. I had a mass of black hair, weighed eight and a half pounds, and my looks favoured my father's family. My maternal grandmother Amelia was an early visitor, but it seems she ignored me. Mother, hurt by her mother's indifference, said,

"She's a lovely little darkie, aren't you going to look at her?"

"Oh, I quite forgot the bibee!" said Granny.

No doubt my mother was biased, but she loved to tell how every one admired her babies. My sister Peggy, who was seventeen months older than me, and a blonde blue-eyed beauty, rode at the foot of the big old-fashioned pram, while I, the newly-born child, with jet black hair, lay at the hooded end.

Each day my mother pushed her precious cargo some five miles; it seems that every one she met complimented her on the beauty of her children. Daily she returned home to make tea for her young husband, glowing with pride and happiness.

A few months before she died at nearly ninety-five years of age, she recalled those days and with tears brightening her tired blue eyes said, "I was so happy then . . ."

But Dorothy's complete happiness was not to last for long. The Utopian era soon passed.

A third pregnancy occurred; I do not know exactly how long after my birth. At a late stage of my mother's waiting time, a young friend woke my parents in the early hours of the morning, by throwing stones against their bedroom window. The friend was calling for help for his wife who was in labour with her first child. The midwife engaged to deliver the baby had not arrived, delayed it seems, by the extreme weather. It was discovered later that she had broken her leg in a fall on the icy roads.

Dorothy walked through deep snowdrifts to attend the young mother, and delivered the baby unaided. But the shock of being woken in the dead of night by pebbles raining on the windowpane caused the baby she was carrying, in my mother's words, to "lurch in my womb". From that time, the baby did not move and my mother became very ill. Eventually she was delivered of a stillborn girl.

Peggy and I were blissfully unaware of this unhappiness. Our paternal grandmother, Elizabeth, looked after us, and no doubt we were thoroughly spoiled by the aunts and uncles who still lived in the family home.

The next crisis arose when Peggy and I both developed whooping cough. It was long before the days of inoculations, and in common with other children of the time we were very ill indeed. Antibiotics were still decades away, and children just had to endure constant coughing and vomiting for one whole winter. Our parents took turn and turn about to sit with us through the nights, and every morning there was, in my mother's words, "a bath full of washing" to be done.

In these days of electric washing machines, it is hard to appreciate the amount of work involved in dealing with "a bath full of washing". To produce hot water and "to boil" the wash, mother had to start a fire with paper and sticks under the brick copper in the corner of the kitchen.

All through my school days, I recall the ordinary week's wash taking the whole week to complete. All day Monday the kitchen floor would be awash with the

3

overflow from tubs of soapy water, boiling, blueing, starching and wringing. On Tuesday the task was drying and "folding down". Wednesday and Thursday would be taken up with ironing, using a pair of old-fashioned flat-irons, each of which had to be heated in turn on the gas cooker. On Friday there was still the airing and putting away to be done.

The little folk song, sung by the children of the day was based on fact:

> T'was on a Monday morning,
> That I beheld my darling,
> She looked so sweet and charming oh,
> In every high degree.
> She looked so neat and nimble oh,
> A-washing of her linen oh,
> Dashing away with a smoothing iron,
> Dashing away with a smoothing iron,
> She stole my heart away.

And so on through, Tuesday, drying; Wednesday, folding; Thursday, ironing and Friday, airing.

Soon after the whooping cough winter, Peggy and I were running ahead of our parents when we managed to get our legs tangled together and fell. According to mother, I cried all night after this little accident, and the next morning my arm was "as big as a lamp post". When I eventually reached the hospital, the green stick fracture had set itself, and I have the resulting lump on my right elbow to this day. The arm was in plaster for eight weeks, and I had to be pushed several times a week to the hospital, which was situated some four miles from home.

Another happening, which occurred before school days, was the removal of my tonsils. It was a common enough practice in those days, and I am told that I was much better for it, although I have to say I have been troubled with "tonsillar remnants" ever since.

In the 1920s it was believed that parental visits to children in hospital served only to upset the child. Tiny infants were deposited with nursing staff, then mother was whisked away, not to be seen again by the child until he or she was ready to return home. I remember being left with a little teddy bear, told to be a good girl and not to cry. When the day for returning home eventually came, my mother found me sitting in my cot clothed in a vomit-stained nightdress; I looked up at her and said, "I didn't cry, Mummy." But I'm told there was never a child nearer to tears, without actually crying.

To complete the four or five fraught years, Peggy then had her tonsils removed.

By September 1927, the affairs of our little family seemed to have settled down, and my father badly wanted to take us all away on holiday. People from our background did not often indulge in holidays, and mother was not keen on the experiment, preferring the cosy security of home. But Dad's mind was made up, and away we went to spend a week with my mother's brother and his wife in Basingstoke. Not exactly a holiday resort, it may be thought, but old Basingstoke was then quite a pleasant little country town, although

5

in recent years the cottages, malt house and pretty churches have been replaced by a concrete jungle, roundabouts and miles and miles of one-way streets.

I have two images in my mind of the week in Basingstoke. One, Auntie Vi and Uncle Ern taught everyone to dance the Charleston. I mean *everyone*. I suspect that the young adults had a great deal of fun and certainly Peggy and I danced madly the whole time.

The other noteworthy event was that I realised for the first time that there was but one moon, and that the moon we had seen shining over Basingstoke was the very same one that shone over our home. I remember my father carrying me on his shoulders, as we completed the last lap of our journey from the tram stop to our house, and having great trouble convincing me that there was only one moon shining for us all.

I started school in either the spring or autumn of 1927. Of the first few weeks I recall nothing, except crying bitterly in the "babies" toilet building. My embroidered cotton knickers had a complicated system of flaps back and front; the side button holes of the front flaps, and the side button holes of the back flaps all fastened on to the same liberty bodice buttons. I had failed to get all the buttons undone, and was upset, lest some mishap occurred before the garment could be removed. Fortunately, a kind "big girl" came to my rescue.

In October 1927 the Prince of Wales visited Bournemouth. Mother, Peggy and I joined throngs of Bournemouthians in Merrick Park hoping to glimpse and cheer the popular young prince. We arrived home mid-afternoon to find father already home from work, and crouched over the smoky fire he had started in the front room. He was shivering violently although it was not a cold day; he wore his overcoat with the collar turned up and held a glass of hot milk in his shaking hand.

Mother got him into bed and called the doctor. Our handsome, strong father had double pneumonia, and in twelve days, he died. He was just thirty-four.

Mother was devastated, and too heartbroken to attend the funeral. Only the pressing day-to-day needs of her children kept her going. Today we have "magic" antibiotics to fight such illnesses, but in 1927, it seems pneumonia was usually fatal. There was little to be done but wait for the "crisis" which occurred twelve days after the onset of the illness. A few lucky ones then slowly recovered, but for most it was the end.

My father had been a keen sportsman, playing football in the winter and cricket in the summer. Mother always blamed a cricket match which had continued through a brief shower of rain for my father's death; the fielders had carried on playing in their damp shirts.

Ever after my mother fussed and fretted about exposure to damp and cold. The apparent outcome of "catching cold" could in those days be so disastrous, that perhaps it is not surprising that parents aired every garment to cinder dryness, and desperately protected their children from the elements. My mother was haunted all her life by the belief that a damp shirt had

7

caused my father's death.

The — "I was so happy then" — young mother was now a young widow . . . but life had to go on.

TOTTERING BY GENTLY & THE SLOANE CLUB

INVITE YOU
TO AN EXHIBITION TO CELEBRATE 25 YEARS OF

TOTTERING BY GENTLY
'TOTTERINGS IN BLOOM'

In January 1994, Tottering by Gently made its first appearance in Country Life Magazine. Created by Annie Tempest and under the guidance of Raymond O'Shea of the O'Shea Gallery, the Tottering cartoon strip has been developed into an international brand.

As part of the silver anniversary celebrations, we are delighted to announce the largest exhibition of Tottering originals in 25 years, comprising over 400 watercolour cartoons, which will be held at The Sloane Club to coincide with the Chelsea Flower Show.

Alongside this commemorative exhibition, renowned 23-time gold-medal winning English rose breeder, David Austin is unveiling a new rose called Tottering-by-Gently which will also be featured in the Sloane Club garden as part of Chelsea in Bloom's prestigious annual floral art show.

The Tottering-by-Gently rose is a primrose yellow bloom with rich golden stamens and an intriguing fragrance with hints of orange peel. A large shrub, also suitable for hedging, the Tottering-by-Gently rose flowers regularly throughout the summer months.

The TOTTERINGS IN BLOOM exhibition is open to the general public with free admission. Come along and meet the artist who will be creating cartoons throughout the exhibition.

THE SLOANE CLUB, LOWER SLOANE STREET, CHELSEA , LONDON SW1W 8BS
PUBLIC ENTRANCE : CORNER OF LOWER SLOANE STREET AND TURK'S ROW.
TUESDAY 22ND MAY TO SATURDAY 26TH MAY, 2018.
OPEN TO THE PUBLIC FROM 8.30 AM TO 5.00PM

CHELSEA IN BLOOM

Enquiries: lordtottering@hotmail.com   www.tottering.com

COUNTRY LIFE®

EVERY WEEK

Happy Anniversary, Tottering

TOTTERINGS IN BLOOM EXHIBITION
INVITATION OVERLEAF

CHAPTER TWO

Now We Are Three

I well remember how I dreaded Mother meeting her acquaintances. After a few minutes, the conversation naturally turned to our recently departed father and Mother would begin to wipe her eyes and blow her nose. I wished so much that we did not have to stop and talk; it seemed to my young mind that the kind enquirers were causing Mother's grief. I know now that it probably helped to talk. As a child I knew nothing of grief or that it was there all the time. Now I know that suppressed grief produces the most searing pain of all.

The loss was not only devastating; it also meant that our little family now had money problems. As a skilled carpenter, my father had earned a good wage; he was also a self-taught, but gifted, draughtsman and made extra money by drawing plans for local builders. Bournemouth expanded rapidly in the 1920s, and my father had never been short of work. By the standards of the times, we had been a comfortably-off family.

Now, mother's pension was 10/- for herself, 5/- for Peggy and 3/- for me. We lived in a house that belonged to my father's mother, but, like other tenants, we had always paid full rent. The most thoughtful of my father's sisters, Ethel, persuaded my grandmother to allow us to live rent-free. This was truly a godsend and eased our biggest financial problem.

Mother never again slept in the big front bedroom that she had shared with my father, so that was the room chosen to be let to a succession of lodgers, at a rental of 6/- per week.

Of the many people who occupied the big front bedroom, my strongest recollection is of two elderly sisters, Miss Collins and Mrs Leach. They dressed in ankle-length black garments, and a more prim and proud couple could not be imagined. Miss Collins seldom left the house, but Mrs Leach augmented their income by occasionally performing what she called a "dooty" (duty). As a retired nurse, she obtained casual employment sitting with very ill patients through the night. She was immensely proud of her "dooties", and I can see her now as she departed to perform them, a tiny upright figure, dressed in a big old-fashioned hat and a long black skirt.

Despite the loss of father, we had the happiest of childhoods. I look back on years of joy, security and completeness. Mother was one in a million and we lacked nothing. In my father's time there may have been more money to spend on little luxuries. For example, he often took us to the local toy shop on St Peter's Hill and allowed us each to spend sixpence. Once when he returned from an away football match, he arrived home in the early hours of the morning with a toy gramophone and tiny records. He insisted on

NOW WE ARE THREE

waking us (I can imagine how opposed my mother would have been to this), to play the "Laughing Policeman" and the "Laughing Ploughboy" to his delighted audience.

Now there was constant and very careful budgeting, but we always "managed". Our grandmother, "Gan-Gan", helped a lot. We visited her every Sunday morning and always returned home with a bag of fruit and another of chocolate biscuits. Also Mother did a pile of washing for Gan-Gan every week, and she was rewarded with 3/6 for her trouble.

Auntie Florrie conveyed the bundle of washing to our house every Monday morning. On Mondays, she collected the rents of the sixty or so houses owned by Gan-Gan, and could conveniently drop the washing in as she passed. On Fridays the laundered bundle had to be returned. When we became old enough, either Peggy or I had to perform this task, and I hated the world knowing that my mother did washing for payment. No one could be in any doubt as to what the bundle contained, because it was always wrapped parcel-fashion in a piece of old sheeting and secured with two large safety pins.

The state pension, plus the rent from the front bedroom and the washing money, took care of our day-to-day living. All extras, such as clothes and replacements in the home, were provided by the proceeds from summer letting.

Living in a seaside town, there was scope for "bed and breakfast" letting throughout the summer months. At times Mother even undertook "full board", but this made her very, very tired. Single-handedly Mother dealt with the summer visitors and all the cooking, cleaning and shopping involved. Somehow, this had to be fitted in with the usual chores and Gan-Gan's washing.

Guests were obtained by advertising in certain newspapers. Composing the advertisement was a combined effort; usually we started with "Clean comfortable accommodation . . ." We never mentioned that the house was three miles from the sea, but no doubt the quoted price reflected this little inconvenience. Most guests seemed satisfied and came back year after year. I'm sure the food was good and plentiful, for we had lots of "recommendations".

On the day "the people" departed, Peggy and I usually contrived to be sitting in the porch hoping, rather obviously, that a threepenny or sixpenny tip would come our way. Then, as soon as the guests were five or six yards down the road, we dashed up to the vacated bedroom, to see if they had left anything. Not, I hasten to add, with the intention of running after the careless holidaymakers, but hoping for some material gain for ourselves. Mostly, we found only a piece of used soap or an old magazine, but we young treasure hunters never lost our optimism or enthusiasm.

There was one aspect of the letting season that really mortified me. All of the bedrooms being occupied by either permanent or temporary guests, the three of us had to sleep on makeshift beds in the middle downstairs room, the room we called the kitchen. The front downstairs room was earmarked for visitors' dining and lounging, while the third room, known as the scullery, was used to capacity for cooking, washing and family meals. Beds for the three of us had to be wedged into the little kitchen. We were comfortable enough, but I found it embarrassing not to have a room in which to entertain my school friends.

I could not bear my visitors to see the hotch-potch of bedding, and always tried to waylay them before they reached the kitchen. They must have found my conduct extremely odd, since the kitchen was the room we normally used for playing and entertaining. No doubt they guessed what was going on, but somehow I could not bring myself to admit that we were "camping" in the kitchen. It was mean of me to be embarrassed by my mother's hard work and gallant efforts, but without doubt I was embarrassed.

Peggy and I were the principal beneficiaries of the money earned from letting. We were easily the best-dressed children in the school. Mother was very proud, and come what may she was not going to let her children look poor. Although the school did not require that uniforms should be worn, we were always turned out in navy blue serge tunics and white poplin blouses of the very best quality, and modelled closely on those worn by the local grammar school pupils. We were near perfect replicas of the Bournemouth School for Girls fraternity, right down to the black woollen stockings and black-laced shoes. In winter we wore navy nap cloth coats and black velour hats, while in the summer, panama straw hats and navy blazers completed the outfits. We lacked only the official badges. I am sure we could have nipped into the grammar school and passed for *bona fide* pupils — until the register was called.

Our wet weather gear left nothing to chance. Mother certainly did not risk our catching cold or having to sit in damp clothing. In addition to macintoshes worn over the navy nap cloth coats, and sou'westers substituting for the velour hats, our legs and feet were protected either by wellington boots or a combination of gaiters and galoshes. The gaiters were made of thin rubberised fabric and buttoned from knee to ankle with about twenty tiny buttons. Of course, we also carried umbrellas. Imagine the time it took to don all the gear and then, after making the five minute walk to school, taking it all off again!

Our "best" clothes were equally outstanding. Every winter a professional seamstress made us identical coats and a milliner was employed to make hats in matching material. When spring came along, lightweight coats were produced, to be worn for the first time on Easter Sunday. Weekend stockings were in beige coloured wool, and our shoes of good quality patent leather or brown calf. Leather gloves and little handbags completed the outfits. On Whit Sunday, new dresses were worn, always made to identical patterns, but sometimes in different colours. Mother usually made the dresses herself. She did not own a sewing machine and so all the work had to be carried out by hand; the countless hours of patient sewing produced some very creditable results.

My father's sisters had our interests very much at heart, and Auntie Win, who loved knitting, kept us supplied with hand knitted vests. Made in thick wool and two-plain-two-purl rib, they were pulled snugly to the neck with draw strings; the sleeves ended just above the elbow, while the body of the vest was made very long to allow for shrinkage and the wearer's growth. When new, the garments reached well below our knees, and all the extra length had to be tucked as neatly as possible into our knickers. This was achieved by folding the vests to treble thickness round our bottoms. Even now, the thought of those thick itchy vests sets me wriggling and scratching. I've never worn a vest since the control of such matters passed into my own hands!

We possessed bathing costumes in the style of the day, all-in-one garments in dark cotton interlock, bound with white or pale blue. I do not recall entering the water in our costumes, but we were allowed to wear them on very hot days, both on the beach and in the garden at home. However, we always had to wear our vests under the bathing costumes!

CHAPTER THREE

Sundays

On Sunday morning, we bathed in a galvanised bath before the kitchen fire. On one side of the hearth, our clean garments were hung on a chair to air and warm. Each item had to be turned constantly to ensure that it was completely and unquestionably aired. When, eventually, we were dressed and our hair brushed, a suitable interval had to be waited while "our pores closed". Only then, were we permitted to set off on our routine visit to Gan-Gan's house.

Several aunts and uncles still lived at home and they were lovely to us, so we never needed persuasion to make the Sunday morning visit. In addition to the bags of fruit and chocolate biscuits, Gan-Gan never failed to give us a silver threepenny piece each. Generally, this was our only source of pocket money and the subject of careful budgeting.

We had strict instructions not to eat anything during the visit because Mother was at home cooking the Sunday joint, and appetites must not be spoiled. Sometimes, if we had dilly-dallied on the walk home, and had not arrived until after lunch had been "dished up", we would be in moderate trouble. Before we could actually partake of the Sunday roast, all the best clothes had to be removed, only to be donned again when we set out for Sunday School an hour or two later.

Our cousins Phyl and "Big Gwen", who were ten or eleven years older than us and taught at the Congregational Sunday School, undertook to escort us to this happy introduction to things spiritual. I recall the little hall with its rows of chairs in sizes varying from minute ones for the "babies", through several stages, to almost full sized seats for the largest children.

That well known picture of Jesus surrounded by small children, some white, some black and some yellow hung on the wall. I suppose "Suffer the little children to come unto me" was the first Bible quotation I became acquainted with.

We sang "All things bright and beautiful", "Jesus bids me shine with a clear bright light", "The whole wide world for Jesus" and all the lovely old hymns for children. When the time came for our young teachers to tell us Bible stories we divided into small groups. Then we recorded our impressions of the stories in convoluted pictures, drawn with coloured crayons. Finally, collection coppers were rescued from gloves and knicker pockets and placed in the plate.

Some Sundays were special and required that the children bought gifts. For Harvest Festival, cardboard boxes covered with crepe paper were filled with fruit or vegetables. If much at little cost was required, the box would be filled with potatoes. The next day the produce was conveyed to the House Beautiful, a local orphanage. The gifts received at the Egg and Flower service were also donated to the House Beautiful. That is to say, most of the gifts reached the orphanage. An enormously fat girl named Rita Adams once placed her brown paper bag of eggs on her chair when she stood to sing a hymn; after the usual drawn out "Amen", she forgot the eggs and flopped down firmly on the chair. Poor Rita, if she had been a fragile little girl, it would not have been nearly as embarrassing!

Sunday's tea was a great treat because the morning's roast beef had produced a bowl of beautiful dripping to spread on our bread. We especially loved the rich gravy jelly from the bottom of the basin. Sometimes Mother had found time while she was cooking, to rub up a few rock cakes or jam tarts. Sunday tea was certainly something to anticipate and to enjoy.

Quite often we all three went to Church in the evening. The service tended to be boring, but I knew it was good to go and enjoyed the resulting feeling of self-righteousness. As we grew older, the ladies' outfits and hats provided some distraction. The young Sunday School teachers and their boyfriends also received a certain degree of attention, and mental notes were made for discussion later on.

Peggy and I often felt we had got the hang of sermon making, and filled many a half hour standing in front of the mirror which hung over the kitchen fireplace, "preaching" impromptu sermons. They tended to become hilarious. One subject, in no way religious but one on which we could keep going for a very long time, was "The cork is no good without the bottle, and the bottle is very little good without the cork"!

Frequently there was yet another outing on Sunday. The local YMCA held an entertainment described as a "Sacred Concert" at eight-fifteen on Sunday evenings. There was always an "artiste" who sang, played a musical instrument or recited, a speaker and the evening started and finished with a hymn. No charge was made for this enjoyable entertainment but a collection plate was passed round. I suspect that my mother's contribution was coin of the lowest denomination, lowered discreetly into the plate.

The Sunday School made other contributions to our social life. From time-to-time the young teachers, that is to say the three Miss Jeffs, our cousins Phyl and "big" Gwen, and one or two others, produced concerts. The teachers, usually dressed as pierrots, were the stars. Singing and dancing in high-kicking chorus lines, they daringly exposed inches of Celanese knicker-leg as the pianist strummed out, "Tiptoe Through the Tulips", "When You Can't Say a Word You Can Smile" and other popular songs of the day. No doubt the "pictures" and Bournemouth's seaside shows provided the inspiration. A chap named Willie Cave produced a show on the west promenade beach. You had to pay to watch from the rows of deckchairs, but if you stood on the prom, it was free, or you could pop a coin in the bag handed round by one of the pierrots. I suppose Willie Cave's little show was as popular with teenagers then as *Top of the Pops* is for today's youth.

Peggy and I were always rather boringly cast as "fairies" or "flowers". I suppose we were too small to do anything more than hop around the stage. Our cousins made our costumes in coloured crepe paper, decorated with Christmas tinsel. Whatever the outfit we were not permitted to remove our vests, and I well remember the constant battles to keep the vest sleeves out of sight. No matter how many giant safety-pins were used, the sleeves usually won.

I suppose the Sunday School outing was the event of the year. A different venue, usually somewhere in the New Forest, perhaps Burley or Sway, was chosen each year. No charge was made for the pupils, but parents had to pay sixpence each. Mother always found a sixpence for the outing, there was no way she would allow us to go into the wilds of the New Forest unsupervised.

We gathered at the Sunday School hall at about eight o'clock in the morning, eager to clamber onto the coaches for what seemed a long, long journey. Although the chosen day usually proved to be a "scorcher", each child carried a cardigan, a mackintosh and a packed lunch.

We played happily in the selected field all the morning. Sometimes, in our quest for wild flowers we wandered into adjacent fields, but mostly our respect for the unfamiliar wild ponies kept us close to the main party. At midday we sat on our outspread Macs and consumed our sandwiches, adding interest to the fare by making a few "swaps" with friends.

After lunch, the teachers set about organising sports and "scrambles". The teachers threw handfuls of wrapped sweets and we all "scrambled" for them. An adept scrambler could end the day with pockets crammed with sweets. No one indulged in food fads in those days or worried about the effect of sugar on our teeth. But we always cleaned our teeth before going to bed and Mother saw to it that we made visits to the dentist. How thankful I am that my mother was concerned about our teeth. When I joined the WAAF in the forties, many of the young girls had complete sets of false teeth, but I still have my own quite respectable looking teeth today.

The races were even more profitable. We had flat races, egg and spoon, three-legged, relay, potato and sack races. The prizes were always money: thre'pence for winning, tuppence for coming second and a penny for the third past the winning post. I happened to be pretty nimble and always went home much richer than I had arrived.

Tea was provided in a local church hall before tired, dirty, but very happy, we climbed back into the charabanc for the long drive home. Assuring each other that it had been the best "treat" yet, we settled down to sing lustily every mile of the journey home.

CHAPTER
FOUR

Unforgettable Christmas

Christmas was the other unforgettable event of the year. Poor though we were, we were in no way deprived at Christmas.

The festive season started early in November when Messrs Beales, the large local department store, arranged that Father Christmas should "arrive". With his retinue he alighted at the Central Station (having boarded the train at Boscombe Station two miles down the line), then, high on his painted carriage which was drawn by several horses, he paraded through the town to the store. Few children attended school that afternoon. With their mothers, they scrambled onto one of the many extra trams and rushed to claim a place somewhere along the route. There we jostled and pushed for places, and eventually, with much flag waving and genuine enthusiasm, we welcomed the smiling old gentleman.

Those nearest to the store then fought their way into the shop and up to the second floor to queue to receive a present (on production of a sixpenny ticket), from

Santa Claus' own hand as he sat in his Grotto or whatever the store had dreamed up for the year. We usually delayed that part of the proceedings for another day, when we happily did the rounds to see various Father Christmases in all the big shops. All sorts of exciting fantasies were concocted. It could be a ride in an imaginary aeroplane, a trip in a submarine or a quick excursion to Fairy Land. Father Christmas was always found sitting at the end of the ride, ready to ask what you wanted him to bring on the 25th and to hand you your sixpenny toy to be going on with.

We were enterprising children. At the ages of eleven or twelve we discovered a useful way of making extra money for Christmas. We ran Christmas clubs. The plural is correct because we quickly found that by organising three clubs, one in each of our names, we could earn three free gifts. The rate of commission was the same irrespective of the size of the order, therefore, although we worked together to acquire customers, collect the weekly savings, circulate the catalogues and finally distribute the goods, we sent individual orders. The general administration work presented no difficulty, neither did the clerical tasks nor the calculation of the commission. I suspect that we were among Messrs Dyson and Horsefall's most conscientious and efficient club organisers. The excitement on the day the huge wooden crates arrived was tremendous. We spent the evening ankle-deep in sawdust, ticking off the goodies and then sorting them into little piles, ready for delivery to our customers. It was quite good entrepreneurial training for Peggy and

23

me. Mother was just a sleeping partner. Dyson and Horsefall never enquired as to the age of their agents.

Gan-Gan and the aunts and uncles provided most of our presents. Officially, of course, they all came from Father Christmas; in reality, the aunts popped the pile of parcels into the unlocked porch during Christmas Eve evening. From there, Mother placed them under and at the ends of our beds for discovery on the morning of the twenty-fifth. We had truly wonderful presents; we did far better than most of our friends who had fathers. In addition to the big gifts, our stockings were crammed with fruit, chocolates, all sorts of novelties and right at the top there was always a miniature Christmas cake. For years after we realised that there was no Father Christmas we happily went along with the charade, pretending not to hear the porch door being pushed open, the rustle of parcels as they were piled up and the porch door being pulled shut again.

We augmented our own funds for buying Christmas presents by carol singing. Avoiding the houses where we knew dogs were kept, we sang verse after verse to our long-suffering neighbours. It did not occur to us to collect for a charity, other than ourselves. The pennies were carefully hoarded and added to weeks of saved pocket money. Evenings were spent poring over lists as we planned how to spend our few shillings to best advantage, followed, finally, by a joyful visit to Woolworths to obtain the best value possible in gifts for Mother, each other, friends and relatives. Some Christmas cards we made ourselves, but Woolworths sold very good ones for a halfpenny each. We knew people who rubbed out the names on cards they had received the previous year — we never sunk to that!

Our Christmas lunch was a joint of pork or beef, the flavour of poultry being unknown to me until I became a teenager. There was, of course, a pudding of the genuine home-made variety. Peggy and I had been in on every stage of the pudding making, right from the arrival of the ingredients as a gift from Auntie Win. It involved much washing of fruit, grating of peel and suet and hours of stirring; then a whole day steaming the puddings in a giant fish kettle. You could not see across the kitchen on the steaming day, and the walls ran with condensation. But it was all worthwhile and the result delicious.

The rest of Christmas day was spent at Gan-Gan's house. There, money was plentiful and the hearts of Gan-Gan and the aunts generous. The "front" room was in use, its posh "modern" furniture so impressive and luxurious. A patterned carpet square covered most of the floor and the latest style three-piece suite in uncut moquette offered comfort, most marked when compared with our own upright chairs and linoleum-covered floors. Big coal fires roared away in both the "front" and "back" rooms. (The practice of calling rooms "lounge" or "dining" had not reached us.)

In the "back" room the dining table was extended to its fullest size and laden with a huge tea, and later with a gigantic supper. Every imaginable item of Christmas fare was provided, not to mention crackers in many sizes and cotton wool snowballs containing gifts for everyone. Between the meals we adjourned to the "front" room and there we were offered chocolates, nuts, dates and fruit; far more than we could possibly eat. The house in Portland Road was well stocked with drinks too. My uncles certainly liked their tipple, but the womenfolk did not imbibe very much. Peggy and I were provided with raisin wine, a dark sweet liquid which contained no alcohol, but as it was dispensed in little wine glasses identical to those used by the grown-ups, we felt we were very sophisticated.

The aunts played the piano and we all sang; Uncle Reg had a good voice and never seemed to tire of his favourite song "Home, home on the Range". I remember wondering about this Range, where the buffalo roamed and the sky was not cloudy all day! Sometimes we sang "Bye-bye blackbird" and "Among my souvenirs", both of which had been favourites of my father. I watched my mother anxiously for that look of sadness — it was always there.

Long after our normal bedtime, Uncle Reg, who by then was just slightly unsteady on his feet, escorted us home. Once there, the Valour stove would be lit in the kitchen to enable the tired revellers to don their nightclothes in comfort, while Mother popped the kettle on the gas stove to fill the stone hot water bottles.

Christmas was over.

CHAPTER
FIVE

School Days

My school days started a few months before my father's death. I remember little of the first years or of my progress. I think I must have learned to read fairly quickly, because I do not remember ever being unable to read. We did endless "reading round the class", and I was very bad at that. Instead of reading word for word as written on the page, I had the bad habit of reading ahead of myself and transposing words while more or less retaining the sense of the piece. Of course, this did not do; I was corrected by the teacher every few words and labelled a poor reader. However, I became an enthusiastic member of the local library and read endless books. When very young I remember reading of the escapades of boarding school girls, Angela Brazil being a favourite author, then came Mazo De La Roche's "Whiteoak" stories, the tales of Dornford Yates and many others. Unfortunately, I received no guidance whatsoever as to what should be read.

Mother taught us to knit before we started school and we had plenty of practice in the infants' school; almost every afternoon was spent wrestling with nasty pieces of knitting. The needles provided were wooden and rough, and had no "slip" whatsoever; hot sticky little hands had to fight to complete each "in-round-through-off". The resulting grubby little squares were not encouraging.

By the age of eight I had progressed into Miss Gravestock's class in the "Big Girls" department, and was in the "A" stream of two parallel age classes. There, the large grey-haired teacher resolved to teach me a lesson of a not strictly academic kind.

I can imagine how aggravating a child I was. All arithmetic came easily to me, so as Miss Gravestock worked through examples on the blackboard, with hand up I worked my way foot by foot up the aisle between the desks, quite unable to contain my desire to spit out the answer before Miss Gravestock had finished her explanation.

When it came to other subjects, particularly those which did not interest me or come easily to me, I did not bother to attend and giggled away with one or two like-minded children at the back of the class.

At the end of the first year, as nine-year-olds, we were all "put up", but instead of going into the "A" stream class, I found myself in the "B" stream. Thank you Miss Gravestock, I needed someone to say to me "You've got to make an effort even when you don't find the subject riveting. School isn't just for having a riotous giggly time, and you're developing into a cocky bore as far as arithmetic is concerned."

I stayed in class 2B for one term and was then allowed to rejoin the "A" stream.

All figure-related subjects continued to come easily to me and I was usually ahead of my companions. My handwriting and spelling were abysmal. English grammar I just did not and do not understand. (Apparent in these notes no doubt.) I used to get a reasonable mark for the "matter" of my essays, but very low marks for spelling, writing and English.

Nature study, poetry and art were unnecessary rubbish as far as I was concerned. I was good at games and won medals for running and swimming; when eligible I was always in the school netball team.

I think it is fair to say I was quite popular with my companions, but then children who are good at sports usually are. Even so, it was a pleasant surprise when in my final year with the three other House Captains, I faced an election for the position of "Head Girl" and forty-seven of the fifty girls in Standard 7 voted for me.

Education was unimportant to Mother, and I do not recall her pushing us in any way. She wanted us to be the best-turned-out children in the school and I'm sure it mattered that we were pleasant and respectful to our teachers. Most importantly we had to be able to earn a living in due course.

At the age of eleven, all children took the "Scholarship" examination. An average of three or four out of the hundred or so girls from my school who were eligible, would eventually find themselves at either Bournemouth School for Girls, or Bournemouth High School (later to become Talbot Heath School). Both Peggy and I did well enough to pass the written part of the scholarship and to be selected to go forward to the interview stage; then Mother withdrew us because she felt unable to afford the books or the uniform. I think she was also influenced by a wish to have us working and earning from an early age. Attending one of the grammar schools would have meant staying on at school until sixteen or eighteen. We were virtually wearing the uniform already, but no doubt the books would have been expensive. In later years, I wished so much that our generous Grandmother had stepped in and made it possible for us to take up our scholarships.

My school days were happy carefree days without pressure of any kind.

School being just around the corner we always came home to lunch. Mother never failed to have a wholesome meal awaiting us. The only menu I recall was Monday's cold meat and "bubble and squeak" (left over potato and cabbage mashed together and fried), followed by rice pudding. An easy meal, because Monday was "washday" and the morning had been fully occupied with scrubbing, boiling, starching and wringing. At lunchtime the fire under the copper in the scullery would still be crackling away, the room full of steam and the floor awash.

Most days, after lunch, we moved into the "front" room for a sing-song round the piano. We sang hymns, traditional songs such as "Clementine", "Londonderry Air", "Men of Harlech", as well as all the popular songs of the day: "Amy" (about Amy Johnson the pilot), "Sally" and "Sing as you go" to name a few. One of our school friend's mothers had lived next door to Gracie Fields' family in Rochdale, and claimed that

Gracie's mother did her mother's washing. Perhaps that accounted for our liking for Gracie Fields' songs.

We also sang all the old music hall songs that had originated thirty or forty years earlier. I particularly remember one "selection" of choruses of old time songs that we sang from beginning to end most lunch times. Even now, if I chance to hear one of those music hall numbers, my mind automatically follows on with the next song in the selection. "Daisy Daisy" is followed by "Stop the Cab", then "Skylark", "It's a Great Big Shame" and so on.

I still have all my school reports and have to admit they are full of "could do betters", and my place in class not nearly as high as my recollections suggest.

The teachers I remember very clearly. There was Miss Kent who was reputed to wear a wig. I'm sure she didn't, but all her pupils chose to dally behind her desk, peering closely at her head, hoping to find some evidence to prove the rumour. It was Miss Kent, who, in an attempt to improve my quite horrific handwriting, made me copy lines from what was even then considered to be old fashioned, a Copy Book. I was the only pupil made to do this — I fear it did not have much effect. All Miss Kent's efforts failed to bring style to my handwriting.

Miss Kent was also the school music teacher and organiser-trainer of the choir. From the age of eleven, those who could sing in tune were privileged to become part of the choir. Peggy and I were always members although according to Peggy, who was musical and played the piano well, I did not sing in

31

tune. The choir practised for weeks before taking part in a competition for school choirs at the Bournemouth Music Festival. Miss Kent worked really hard with us and produced some creditable results. We won the shield every year of the four years I was a member of the choir.

The competition took place at the Bournemouth Winter Gardens, made famous by Sir Dan Godfrey. The huge glass building was full of magnificent plants and vines. The grounds were interesting too, having masses of little paths and walks, bridges over tiny ravines, and there were small secret seats and alcoves. The successful competitors in each section took part in a concert in the evening, and since we always won the Girls' School section, we were required to remain around for several hours waiting to perform in the concert. We had the greatest fun scooting round the paths and walks; there was always something new to be discovered.

Special dresses, made in the school colours and from identical patterns, were worn for the choir competition; but some of the mothers were indifferent needlewomen and the resulting dresses not quite as the pattern intended. Perhaps the quality of our singing made up for our less than immaculate appearance.

In states of high tension, we sang our "part" and our "unison" songs, then sat with sweating hands and much bitten lips, while the adjudicators summed up and awarded the marks.

According to custom, when we were announced as winners, Miss Kent gave the Head Girl a nod which said "walk up to the platform and collect the shield".

Amid cheers and enthusiastic hand clapping, the Head Girl walked through the great hall, climbed on to the stage and graciously received the shield.

In the fourth year of my choir membership, I was Head Girl and eagerly anticipated the honour and limelight of receiving the shield. It was a great disappointment to me that when the moment arose, Miss Kent broke with tradition and gave another girl the necessary "nod".

Mother loved classical music and in earlier days when she could afford to do so, attended many of the concerts of the Bournemouth Symphony Orchestra under Sir Dan Godfrey. She considered the day of the choir competition one of the highlights of her year, and she continued to attend for many years after we had grown up and left home. Mother was an able piano player, although I believe she had only a year or so of tuition. She bought her piano when she was a girl of eighteen, and throughout her long life it was her most cherished possession. Peggy played very well and was said to have a nice "touch". Unfortunately, I refused to take lessons. (How we regret these things in later life.) I remember attending just one lesson. The teacher started by telling me that the spaces on the music score were F.A.C.E., and asked what FACE spelt. I was only five or six years old and had no idea what FACE spelt. It seems I was too embarrassed to return for further lessons.

At one time Mother thought that I had a good singing voice and paid for me to take private singing lessons. The lessons continued for a year or so I think;

I do not remember why they came to an end. Peggy had to play for my practice sessions and she complained that I got sharper and sharper! Perhaps she was right, but my teacher did not complain. However I have had a complex about my singing ever since and even in church I am careful not to let anyone hear my voice.

One of my favourite teachers was Miss Stroud. I was with her for two years; at the end of standard 5A she moved with us to 6A. Unlike today's teachers Miss Stroud believed that competition was good for children, and every week our marks were added and we moved around the class according to our scores, starting with the top girl in the front of the row of desks on the left of the room, through to the bottom girl at the back of the row of desks on the extreme right.

My marks for most subjects were mediocre, but Miss Stroud had a wonderful system for awarding the arithmetic marks, which enabled me to get very close to the top of the class every week. After completing the "test" of eight sums and getting them marked as correct, we could go on to complete as many sums as possible in the allotted time. The textbook was full of sums and I was quick and accurate; under this scheme I could usually quadruple my arithmetic marks within the set time. I enjoyed those two years swanning in the top "block", although my reports for the period confirm that it was not a true reflection of my overall ability.

Another young teacher, Miss Campion, died whilst I was a pupil. Although we were spared the details of her illness, I believe she was a victim of TB (tuberculosis) which was the scourge of the times.

Before I left school I became the head of Elliot House and vice captain of the school netball team. I have a photograph of the netball team, and my daughters consider that the girls look a bunch of real toughies; but in fact they were super girls and I could tell a tale about each of them. They were: Edna White (goalkeeper), Phylis Parsons (centre), Marjorie Nippard (attacking centre), Joyce Farley (shooter), Cynthia Clark (defending centre), Marjorie Greenaway (defence), and me (attacking shooter).

I enjoyed all physical activities. We did a lot of country dancing, often giving displays. It was all great fun, especially when the class country dancing went wrong. It's hilariously funny trying to sort out a set country dance which has gone to pieces.

When I was about twelve I was given a little duty which I performed willingly enough, and on which I have looked back with interest and pleasure in recent years. My great-grandmother Charlotte (my father's grandmother) lived in one of Gan-Gan's houses near the school. She was then about eighty years of age and confined to her bedroom. Her bachelor son Tom lived with her, but he worked all day and my great-grandmother depended on various relatives calling to make her a drink at lunchtime.

I was elected to call on Thursdays on my way back to school after lunch. It was a simple task — I had to boil a tiny quantity of water on the gas cooker, pour it on the Bovril already measured in her cup, and take the drink upstairs to Charlotte. She was such a pretty little old lady and so delightfully interesting. We talked mainly about the Royal Family, because she knew just everything about them, and could have interested me for far longer than those few minutes each week. But I got to know her well and really loved her.

Her son, my great-uncle Tom, kept their home spotlessly clean and there was never a thing out of place. The draining boards, tables and in fact most of the furniture seemed to be topped with deal, and scrubbed white.

Years later when I became interested in family history, I learned quite a lot about Charlotte. How she was married at eighteen, widowed at 31 and left with eight children. How she resolved that her children were not going to "go on the parish" and how she worked from morning to night to feed them and to bring them all up to be worthy and respected citizens.

CHAPTER
SIX

Home and a few Catastrophes

We had heaps of friends and they were always made welcome at home. Home was very clean, but not smart or particularly tidy. The floors were covered with well-washed linoleum, plus hearthrugs, little slip mats in front of every door and rugs beside the beds. The best furniture was in the "front" room; the piano of course, and an oak dining room suite mainly for the convenience of the summer visitors. The kitchen, which was the room we lived in, held a large deal-topped table, well scrubbed then covered with a chenille-patterned tablecloth. All our chairs were of the dining variety, hard and upright.

For heating, we depended on coal fires and a Valour oil stove. In the winter, Mother was always up in time to get the fire going before we came downstairs. Our night attire, pyjamas which we always termed our "night suits", was kept in the kitchen cupboard. Dressing and undressing took place in front of the kitchen fire.

I was, I think, ten or eleven before electricity was installed in Evelyn Road. Before that time we depended on gas for lighting and cooking. There were no pilot lights, therefore, when we planned to arrive home after nightfall, matches, a most essential commodity, had to be left where Mother could "put her hand on them"; we all stumbled through the house until she succeeded in "putting her hand" on the matches, then by the flickering light of successive matches she navigated her passage to the centre of the kitchen. A little chain had to be pulled to start the flow of gas, until — usually with about the third match held against the mantle — the room was flooded with yellow light. The mantles were always breaking, making what Mother called a "poor" light, and frequently too much air got into the gas pipe, causing the apparatus to pop and splutter.

Gas was also piped to the upstairs rooms, but was seldom used because each night the gas had to be turned off at the meter for safety reasons. We found candles quite adequate for upstairs use. The gas was paid for by a penny in the slot meter, and it could be very trying if the gas started to "go down", and Mother's purse could not be found quickly.

We had a wireless set and listened to excellent Children's Hour programmes, my strongest recollection being of Richard Goolden's "Castles of England" series. I believe he also took part in a series about Larry the Lamb. Apart from these the only really compelling programmes I remember were boxing matches. We always stayed up late to listen to the big fights and all three of us got in states of frenzy as we followed the fortunes of Freddie Mills and Tommy Farr.

Our wireless set was powered by "accumulators", which had to be recharged every few days. Often enjoyment of a favourite programme was marred by realisation that the accumulator was "going". If the accumulator was swung about on the ten-minute walk to the local wireless shop, the acid would splash out of the battery on to your legs. This was not strong enough to harm the skin, but often burnt unwelcome holes in woollen stockings.

The room that today would be called the kitchen, we knew as the scullery. It was quite a large room containing an old-fashioned ware sink and wooden draining board; in the corner was the brick copper with its fire cavity and a large black kitchen range completed the equipment. The last named was never used during our childhood days. According to my mother, half a hundredweight of coal was needed to get the range started and therefore could not possibly be afforded. Our bath water was heated either in the copper or in buckets on the gas cooker. It then had to be conveyed dangerously to a zinc bath in front of the kitchen fire, or after we had reached the ages of eleven or twelve, up the stairs to be tipped into the bathroom bath.

After we had both started work we did light the kitchen range on a few occasions, and found that it heated the water very efficiently. How much fuel was used I do not recall.

One of the first purchases Peggy and I made when our earnings became reasonable was a gas geyser for the bathroom. It was still in place when my mother died in 1985, some 48 years on. The estate agent who dealt with the sale of the house considered it a museum piece.

We lived in the middle room which today would be called the dining-room, but as previously mentioned was known to us as the kitchen. There we sat on hard chairs round the large deal table for our meals, turning the chairs to sit close to the fire when we relaxed. Mostly I had my nose buried in a book and read with complete concentration that I wish I could achieve today. Apparently, Mother and Peggy had a job to break into my world, and even when they made mind-stirring statements like "Here's a shilling for you Gwen", I remained completely engrossed. I expect my subconscious knew it was not a genuine offer.

The little iron fireplace had a mantelpiece that held a clock. The clock was cheap and had to be wound every night then carried upstairs for bedroom use. I have to confess that I was often to be found in a very unladylike pose with my feet on the mantelpiece. This warmed a large portion of my rear and was exceedingly comfortable.

The "front" room, with its good furniture was only used by the summer visitors or when we had friends to tea. The fireplace was larger and grander than the kitchen model, and according to my mother "gave a wonderful heat". A very respectable clock graced the mantelpiece. The oak dining room suite was my mother's pride and joy; extending oak table, four Rexene-covered dining chairs, two "carvers" and a sideboard. Also, of course, the iron-framed piano piled high with music and the source of so much entertainment, lived in the "front" room. Spotless net curtains were hung at the three windows that made the bay; if any of our visitors indulged in smoking the curtains had to be washed, as Mother could not stand the smell of cigarette smoke. The floor was covered with linoleum until we were in our teens, when Mother bought a very prestigious carpet square.

Upstairs, of course the big front bedroom was always let. For years after Mother was first widowed, all three of us slept in the middle bedroom. Peggy and I took turns to share the "big" bed with Mother, while the other child slept in a little camp bed alongside. This arrangement continued until we were quite big children, until in fact I one day expressed a wish to have a room of my own, and was permitted to move into the small third bedroom. I was nervous, but thrilled to have a room to myself.

We had a bathroom with a toilet upstairs. There was no washbasin but at some stage we did acquire a little cupboard with a space for a round enamel bowl at the top. Mother often "did up" the bath with varying degrees of success. Sometimes the "Bath Enamel" she used developed nasty little ridges. We had an outside toilet as well until something went wrong with it, and Mother had it removed because there was no money to have it repaired.

Our large garden was completely uncultivated, but a lovely place for play. Often, half the children of the road were invited in. All had a riotous time, because there was nothing whatsoever to spoil.

One popular game was netball. A zinc bath with a hole extending halfway over its bottom was perched upside down on the top of the clothesline post, to become the "net". The available children were divided into two teams and a fiercely fought game played, both sides shooting into the same net (zinc bath).

I remember one or two catastrophes which occurred, and which seemed at the time to be earth-shattering tragedies from which we might well not recover.

One day Mother, Peggy and I met Miss Knight, the lady who delivered our newspaper, in Coronation Avenue. We stopped Miss Knight and made the weekly payment. When we arrived home, for some reason Mother looked in her purse and immediately discovered that in carrying out the street transaction, a ten shilling note had been lost.

We all rushed back to the spot where we had stood, and searched and searched, but no ten shilling note could be found. Bearing in mind that our total weekly income was 27/6, the loss of 10/- was a mortal blow. Our poor mother was in such a state, and so were we. I worried about it for weeks and weeks, it seemed that our finances would never recover.

Another catastrophe occurred when Miss Cole, an occupant of the front bedroom, tipped the contents of her stone hot water bottle into the lavatory basin. The bottle slipped from her hands and crashed into the porcelain taking a large chunk out of it.

"Whatever has happened?" screamed my mother, as she rushed up the stairs. She soon discovered what had happened because the water from the lavatory basin was pouring on to the lino. For some inexplicable reason Mother then flushed the lavatory; the entire contents of the cistern escaped through the gaping hole, along the landing and cascaded down the stairs. Harsh words were exchanged. It was fairly easy to mop up the water because there were no carpets to contend with, but the expense of having a new toilet basin fitted was an awful problem. Fortunately, we still had the outside "convenience" at that time.

Another problem, which recurred every winter, was that of freezing water pipes. The house was snug enough if you sat six inches away from the kitchen fire, but this was the only heat and not very useful in terms of keeping the plumbing free from ice. Oh dear. As we grew older, we learnt how to deal with the problem. My method was to turn off the water at the stopcock, then leaving the main tap turned on, drain all the water from the tank in the roof. It worked and we didn't have frozen pipes, but oh! the trouble we had getting the air locks out of the pipes every morning.

As a child I was very nervous of fire. We do not appear to have heard of fire insurance, and the thought of our home going up in flames was the most horrific possibility to me. I worried so much about a disastrous fire, I suppose because I could not see how we would ever get another home if the worst happened. Perhaps the council would have housed us. I do not know. Certainly there was no DSS waiting to take over.

Sometimes on wild wet windy nights Mother would say, "I'm sorry for the people sleeping under the hedges tonight." I suppose people really did sleep under the hedges sometimes, although there was always the workhouse.

To get back to my fear of fire; we depended on our Valour stove and our one coal fire. In the winter the kitchen fire was burning brightly before Peggy and I descended the stairs, then while we were at school, it was banked up with dampened coal dust to burn slowly all day. When teatime came the fire was poked into cheery brightness and we spent our evening sitting, all three of us, as close to the grate as we possibly could. We all went to bed at the same time; whether it was a case of Mother going to bed early, or Peggy and me going to bed late, I do not know. A little of each I suspect. Mother never wanted to be left downstairs alone.

Before I could be persuaded to climb the stairs I always "played up" until water was thrown on the dying embers. Not one tiny glowing coal could be left; the fire was doused every night with kettle after kettle of water, making an unbelievable mess. Equally, I was terrified of possible chimney fires. The chimney was swept every spring (and a great upheaval that was too), but I still became frantic if the flames happened to leap high in the grate.

CHAPTER SEVEN

Friends and Pets

As I was nine or ten before I joined the Brownies and old for a beginner, I quickly rose through the ranks to become "Sixer" of the Pixie Six. We had a wonderful Brown Owl, a Miss Dorothy Moore, who taught us lots of Brownie lore and skills for general living. Later I became a Girl Guide and did all the usual things, including camping in the grounds of the ruined Lulworth Castle. Eventually I returned to the Brownies as a Pack Leader.

At Dudsbury in Dorset, extensive grounds and a modern building were available to the Guides and Brownies of the district. On one occasion, this was the setting for a pageant representing Dorset through the ages. With many others, I was cast as a Norman soldier. We were dressed in chain mail made from painted dishcloths, cardboard helmets and we carried cardboard shields. I have a photograph of four of the Norman soldiers, in which it is difficult to identify the players because the cardboard visors almost completely covered our faces. Despite this, years later when I was in the nursing home for Sarah's birth, another new mother said, "I remember you, you're one of the Norman soldiers in a snapshot I've got at home."

When I was a small girl my very best friend was Beryl Fuller. The Fuller family came to live in one of the semi-detached houses at the end of the road when Beryl and I were about seven years old. The family had moved from Devon and all spoke with a lovely soft Devonshire brogue. Beryl had two brothers and one sister: Tommy aged about three, Joan who was two and Georgie who was just a baby. Poor Beryl had to help her mother a great deal and always had rough work-worn hands. Beryl's Aunt Polly was only three or four years older than Beryl and the source of much interesting information about the "facts of life".

The Fuller parents collected Father Christmas goodies in their locked front room, but Beryl knew where the key was kept, and so arranged to inspect each new purchase as it arrived. During the weeks preceding Christmas, as soon as Mrs Fuller left the house we both dived into the front room and examined every item most carefully. Interesting for me but it must have made Christmas morning a bit tame for Beryl.

Beryl was a tall, pretty girl with naturally curly brown hair, but she was always tired and those poor hands so rough and ingrained with grime — sad to see in a seven-year-old child.

When we were about nine or ten the Fuller family moved away, but another family moved into the road and a new friend came into my orbit. The Adams family bought a detached house near the end of the road, on the hill.

Mr and Mrs Adams were much older than most of the parents we knew, Mr Adams being around seventy and already retired. Mrs Adams, who appeared to be in her fifties, was the most practical and old-fashioned woman I had ever met. She was tall, kindly and without doubt a most excellent mother.

Strangely, I remember more clearly than anything her pendulous bosom that seemed to me to reach to a point about three inches below her waist. Apart from Irene, who became my friend, the family consisted of fourteen-year-old Peggy and John, who was about thirteen.

The Adams home was filled with plain heavy furniture, all, even the beds, made by Mr Adams. It was a beautifully clean and well-run home. The children were always neatly dressed, but mostly they wore hand-me-downs, and their garments were often made out of material that had started life in some other way.

Irene was small, elfin and frail. I remember her in a pale blue beret, many sizes too big for her; her tiny white face almost lost under the huge hat. Her neat grey coat with its cosy fur collar had obviously started out as an adult's coat, but had been carefully remade to fit Irene's small frame.

In the way that opposites sometimes do, Irene and I hit it off from the start. I don't know why, perhaps we both happened to need a friend. I loved sports, while Irene could not catch a ball if her life depended on it and her sprinting ability was nil. However, she was a rewarding pupil at school, working hard and consistently and always obtaining high marks in every subject.

Sometimes we played in Irene's house or garden, sometimes in mine. Mrs Adams could be relied upon to produce good teas when we played there. She was I think, slightly jealous of the rather grand outfits which Peggy and I wore, and once referred to me as being all dressed up "like a fourpenny ha'penny ham bone". It was not until I checked with Mother later that I realised that it was a derisory remark.

Beryl, through the almost adult Auntie Polly, had provided some initial information about the "facts of life". Irene and I pursued the subject further and began to get a more or less accurate picture of what went on. My mother took a magazine called *The Woman's Companion*, and left it lying about, we thought possibly for our benefit. Even so, we were careful to read it only when unobserved. The very personal letters that readers sent to the magazine's doctor quite amazed us. Mother didn't provide any real information, but she often referred to the terrible and awful prospects of the girls who in some hideously shameful way, managed to get themselves pregnant. We understood that the shame experienced by their unfortunate families was worse than death itself. I could not think why they allowed themselves to get pregnant. No one let on that there was any temptation involved or any pleasure in the act. We thought they were just stupid and disgusting.

Anyway, when they were about seven months pregnant, they were whisked away to a home for "fallen" women, where they stayed until after their babies were born and safely adopted.

The families usually made up some story about the girl having been staying with her "auntie" for a while. We all knew the truth of the matter and when, in time, the sad-eyed girls tried to pick up the threads of life again, their shame was never forgotten.

Peggy and I were always very aware of the unfortunate and disadvantaged of this world. Our prayers, apart from the Lord's Prayer and "Gentle Jesus" ended with an ever-growing list of supplications for "the sad, the lonely, the sick, the worried, the disabled and so on". It took quite a long time to recite it all, as we frequently thought of yet another group to add to our list. Then there were the people we mentioned by name. We didn't have to know the people concerned, anyone mentioned in the newspaper or on the wireless was included. Any pet we happened to have at the time also got a mention.

We were never without a canary, and although the bird must of necessity have been replaced from time to time, and its sex was always a mystery, every bird was known as "Joey". By day, in good weather, the cage was placed in the porch, while at nightfall the cage was carried back into the kitchen where it was covered with a cloth, and Joey ceremoniously bidden "Goodnight". For years we also had a tabby-cum-tortoiseshell cat named Winkie, so the day ended with "Goodnight Joey, goodnight Winkie", a phrase which rolls off my tongue very naturally to this day. Winkie could be trusted with the bird and often dozed beside Joey's cage in the porch. People passing the house stopped and gazed in amazement at the unlikely companions.

From time to time Winkie produced a litter of kittens. The maternity ward was always the outside toilet, where a cardboard box was balanced on the lavatory seat for the event. Mother and babies would have been in a draught from the ill-fitting door if the box had been left on the floor. We found good homes for the kittens; they were never destroyed. Once when we arrived home from a YMCA Sacred Concert, a chorus of frantic mewing greeted us and we discovered that several kittens had slipped through the tiny space between the cardboard box and the lavatory seat. All were rescued and the tiny scraps of life dried before the kitchen fire. Anxiously watched and tended by the three of us and Winkie.

In my father's time we had kept dogs. One, an Airedale, was buried in our wild overgrown garden. His grave could always be located because there was a seven or eight inch indentation to mark the spot. Often I sat in this hollow oblong and pretended that it was a boat and that I was sailing on the high seas.

Someone gave us a couple of rabbits on one occasion, but like most children, we tired of looking after them, and finally it was Mother who in the depth of winter had to trudge through the long wet grass to feed the poor things.

So the happy carefree days quickly passed. Underprivileged in some ways, but nonetheless aware of a code for living, which, while it was to restrict us, would also guide us "over life's tempestuous sea". We were simple enough to consider a visit to the pictures to see Tom Walls and Ralph Lynn or Gracie Fields a tremendous treat. A sixpenny ticket for Mother and two fourpenny ones for Peggy and me bought three hours of real pleasure, not every week, but perhaps three or four times a year. The coloured matches Mother threw in the air, while we watched from the warmth of the kitchen, sufficed for our November 5th celebrations, and pleased us mightily.

Today we would be dubbed a single-parent family, but then, in the twenties and thirties we did not consider ourselves disadvantaged in any way. Our mother was one in a million, and we were secure and happy.

CHAPTER EIGHT

Out Into The Big World

I left school at the end of July 1936, while Irene's parents decided to let her stay on for two additional terms. She was young for her age and I am sure they were right to do this. During the two extra terms, Irene had private lessons in typing and shorthand. Her excellent parents made sure that each of their children was equipped to venture into the world.

I too had a wonderful mother, but just as she had not been interested in achievement at school, so she was in no way career minded. I had a good reference from school, with special remarks about my abilities with figures and logic, but it did not occur to my mother to look for work where I could use my natural talents. The first job that came along for her daughter was that of junior shoe saleswoman with a famous shoe retailer, and so in early August 1936, dressed in a long brown crepe dress which was cut on the cross and quite unsuitable for an athletic youngster, I started my shoe selling career.

The staff at the Bournemouth emporium of the famous shoe retailer consisted of Mr Barnes the manager, Miss Matthews first sales, errand boy Mills (Christian name unknown and never mentioned) and me the junior saleswoman. My salary was agreed at 10 shillings per week, plus a penny in the shilling commission on "sundries" sold. The hours were quite outrageous: Mondays, Tuesdays and Thursdays, 9am to 7pm; 9am to 1pm on Wednesdays, 9am to 8pm on Fridays and 9am to 9pm on Saturdays. In the summer months, at the manager's discretion, we usually stayed open yet another hour on Friday and Saturday. After deducting the hour spent in the dingy basement at lunchtime, the working week was therefore 52 or 54 hours according to the season of the year. Fairly tough for a young girl!

I had loved school. I loathed my job. When not busy selling shoes, the junior was required to dust shoeboxes. Day after day I dusted the same boring lot of boxes while the long hours ticked slowly away.

It was marginally better when we were busy. Indeed on the very first morning of my selling career and without any training whatsoever, I was thrown in at the deep end. Normally Miss Matthews approached the first female customer with a smiling "Can I help you Madam?" while Mr Barnes advanced on the first male customer or the second lady to enter the shop, Mills took on the second gentleman or the third lady, and I, to begin with at least, only took customers when every one else was busy.

Starting as I did in August, my first morning brought a rush of trade. Visitors who had arrived in Bournemouth the previous Saturday had, by Monday,

53

discovered that the sultry Bournemouth climate played havoc with the feet. Monday mornings found them queuing to buy something cheap and comfortable. So on the first day of my working life, without any patter, skill or know-how of any kind, I sold a number of unsuspecting customers their holiday shoes.

In those days customers expected expert knowledge, and a great deal of service. The customer's own shoes had to be unlaced, carefully removed and each foot measured. Then with the help of a shoehorn, the masses of possible buys were eased on to each foot in turn. I did my best, but made a pretty poor job of it; when it came to parcelling the purchases, well! I had no idea at all; there was no sliding the shoes in a carrier bag. Every box had to be packed in brown paper with corners neatly mitred and then tied with string.

Most of the time we were not so outrageously busy; I just kept on dusting boxes and observing Mr Barnes and Miss Matthews, this being the approved method of learning the skills of the trade. Finding the specified style was the most difficult part of the job. Despite all the careful foot measuring, we were prepared to sell the customers anything they were foolish enough to buy. I was told never to let a customer walk out of the shop without making a purchase. If I could not produce shoes to please, I had to call Miss Matthews or Mr Barnes. They then checked through the range I had offered, and found other possibilities. When both my seniors were busy, it was sometimes very difficult to keep the customer from leaving the shop, without physically restraining them. Somehow, they had to be persuaded to stay. We were all very depressed if our combined efforts failed to produce a sale.

We were always mindful of the penny in the shilling commission on sundries. After each shoe sale we tried to flog a few sundries. The patter was, "Can I interest you in our special line in hosiery? These stockings sell at 1 shilling a pair and we find that they are very popular." Or, "It's important that you use the correct cleaner on the shoes you have chosen, you will find this cleaner brings them up beautifully."

After all my efforts, my commission, usually less than a shilling a week, was a welcome addition to my funds. As I was allowed to keep a shilling out of my 10 shilling wage and all my commission, I considered myself to be quite well off. Of course, Mother fed and clothed me out of the 8/10 she retained from my wage packet. (The insurance stamp cost 2d a week.)

Mother bought me a brand new bicycle (£5), and so there were no fares to pay and my expenses were few. No doubt the three-mile cycle ride night and morning provided a welcome ration of fresh air and exercise. At the time I did not feel unjustly treated, but looking back from the standpoint of the nineteen-eighties and even allowing for inflation, between one and two shillings for 52 hours of work does seem akin to slave labour.

Mr Barnes, who lived with his wife and teenage children above the shop, was a little man with twinkling eyes and quick movements. As I had led a very sheltered life and my knowledge of what went on

in the world was limited, I was shocked to find that Mr
Barnes had one or two strange habits. He liked to serve
ladies in general, and certain ladies in particular.
Whether Miss Matthews was free or not, Mr Barnes
always rushed forward when one of the "certain" ladies
came into the shop. Then as he manoeuvred the
customer's foot into the shoe, he lifted her foot and leg
very high (remember he was sitting on the low shoe
fitter's stool) and looked long and hard up her skirt. I
could not believe that any man would do such a thing!
Miss Matthews first pointed out this little failing and
thereafter my attention strayed from the box dusting,
as I surreptitiously watched my manager's antics. He
peeped away every time he served a lady, and what is
more, most of the ladies knew what he was doing, and
even more surprising they didn't seem to mind! In fact,
the "certain" ladies, and some of the miscellaneous
ladies, appeared to revel in the operation, so much so
that they were moved to try on shoe after shoe, until
the floor was just littered with discarded footwear. I
was amazed; but something inside me began to get the
message and I started to understand why he behaved
thus.

Miss Matthews was 23 and engaged to a milkman
named Tom. Tom usually came to meet Miss
Matthews and the three of us rode our bicycles home
together. I lived about threequarters of a mile beyond
Miss Matthews's home, so for two and a quarter miles
we cycled along three abreast. No one seemed to think
it was dangerous that we were taking up the whole of
the left hand side of the main road.

Miss Matthews's main interest was her forthcoming marriage and she spoke of little else. Marriage was for me as distant as the moon, just something that people who were getting on a bit indulged in. I just missed my school friends and my netball matches and found the predilections of Mr Barnes and Miss Matthews very strange.

My Wednesday half-day was of little use to me because many of my old friends were still at school, and those who had left school for the most part had Saturday for their half-day. My long hours took all my energy, leaving me a bored, tired and unhappy child.

One little trauma of my shoe shop days remains firmly in my mind. We had been very busy and the floor was littered with shoes. When the floor was finally cleared, it was discovered that I had managed to send a customer away with two odd shoes. High heeled, high fashion, blue suede shoes, one size 5 and one size $6^{1}/_{2}$ had found their way into the customer's parcel.

We did not tell Mr Barnes; we hoped he would not be taking notice when the customer returned having discovered the horrible mistake. But no one returned to have the matter put right. Perhaps the purchaser had two oddly sized feet and had manoeuvred the mistake!

I was intensely worried lest Mr Barnes discovered the box containing the remaining size 5 and $6^{1}/_{2}$ because when that happened, being well indoctrinated by Angela Brazil's books of schoolgirl honour, I would have to own up.

Eventually with the help of Miss Matthews, the

offending pair of shoes was tucked away with a lot of other weird old shoes and stockings that were only brought onto the shelves at stocktaking time. Eventually they were bound to be discovered. I worried and worried, day and night. Eventually my kind mother could stand my nerve-ridden state no longer and produced the 12 shillings and 11 pence for me to purchase the useless "pair" of shoes. In time, my mother sold the shoes to a second hand clothes shop for a shilling or two. I wonder if anyone ever found the second set of odd shoes comfortable?

CHAPTER NINE

Advancement . . . and a Taste of Romance

Irene left school at Easter 1937 and straight away joined the staff of Bowmakers, a large finance company in the centre of the town. She was engaged as a filing clerk, but had been promised that when a vacancy arose, she would be transferred to the typing pool. Irene was paid 12/6 per week and her hours were 9am to 5pm Mondays to Fridays, and 9am to 1pm on Saturdays. It seemed to me that Irene had got it made.

In August 1937 Irene kindly mentioned to me that another filing clerk was required by Bowmaker Ltd.. It took no time at all to consider this interesting piece of intelligence and to apply for the position; joy of joys I got the job. How delighted I was to give Mr Barnes a week's notice of my intention to leave the scene of his peep show, Miss Matthews's wedding talk, and my box dusting labours.

Being on the staff of Bowmakers was like working part time. Added to this there was the company of scores of young people of both sexes to be enjoyed. Saturday afternoons were free and Irene was around to spend them with me. My pay was 12/6 per week and the work a thousand times more interesting than shoe selling. No longer did I eat my sandwiches alone in a dingy basement; Bowmakers had a lovely airy canteen on the fifth floor, where the staff socialised while they enjoyed subsidised canteen meals.

There were seven or eight young people in the filing room; our main task was putting files away alphabetically, and "pulling" them out for the "correspondents" on the staff to deal with. Very easy work for anyone who had mastered the alphabet, and compared with dusting shoe boxes, quite stimulating. The company of six or seven other youngsters made the task almost fun.

In charge was tall, handsome Ivor Cosby who was probably about three or four years older than the rest of us. He just stood around making sure, or at least so we thought, that we got on with the work and did not waste too much time talking and laughing. What we did not know was that his brief was to observe and select one of our number to become "supervisor". I was one of the youngest, being only fifteen, and certainly the most recent recruit, and was therefore surprised to be told a few weeks after commencing work, that I had been selected to become "supervisor". There was no pay increase involved in this promotion; I had to take on the extra responsibility for the same princely sum of 12/6 per week.

I continued to enjoy the work, but was given quite a tough time by some of my companions who, understandably, were a little jealous of my quick promotion. In particular, Irene, as an employee of three months' standing and through whose good offices I had obtained the job, felt a little miffed.

However, Irene did not have to put up with the indignity for long; after a few weeks, she was promoted to the typing pool.

In time, I thought that I too might be considered for a more interesting assignment and asked if I could be transferred to the ledger posting room. My request was granted quite quickly and I found myself in the machine room where customers' accounts were filed numerically and all incoming payments recorded. (Bowmakers was concerned with financing hire purchase.) The juniors were responsible for "pulling" the cards when payments were received and filing them away again after the seniors had made the necessary adjustments on Burroughs ledger posting machines. My ambition was to become a ledger posting machine operator. There was an element of "balancing" the total of money received by the cashiers, with the totals posted, which could involve a lot of investigation and figure work. Just the sort of task that appealed to my fairly logical mind, so I worked hard to become an efficient filer of account cards, with the view to one day gaining promotion to Ledger Posting Machine Operator. The girls in charge of these machines were some of the highest paid employees of Bowmaker Ltd.

So much for work. Perhaps more should be said about play. As I approached my sixteenth birthday I became very aware of the young lads amongst my fellows and it seems they became aware of me.

The first to invite me out was a seventeen-year-old named Walter Perry; for obvious reasons known as "Winkle". I suppose your very first boyfriend just has to be exciting. Winkle was tall, at least several inches taller than my 5 feet 7 inches, sporty, wore glasses, but was not by any standard handsome. To me he might have been Clark Gable when I met him at the Lansdowne for our first outing to the pictures. He had played football that afternoon, but when we met he was smartly dressed in a light grey pinstripe suit, beautifully bathed and shaved, and smelled strongly of pungent Cologne.

I too had taken enormous trouble over my appearance: a recently acquired pale blue costume, white "Hungarian" blouse embroidered in various shades of blue and flat but smart, blue suede shoes.

I remember nothing of the film we saw, but shall never forget the goodnight kiss. It was, as you will have guessed, my first kiss, and the most exciting moment of my life up to that time.

I had two or three giddy dates with Winkle, then for some reason he stopped asking me out. But I did not forget Winkle; wherever or however I spent my Saturday evenings, I always dressed and beautified myself thinking only that I might, just by chance, bump into Winkle. That feeling of anticipation continued for a long time.

But life was not dull in the meantime. A whole succession of boyfriends and dates followed. Cycling home one winter's evening, a lad named Percy Claxton drew alongside me and in precise and measured tones, asked if I would consider going to a dance with him. Percy, who worked for the solicitor attached to Bowmakers, was tall, nice looking and about four and a half years older than me. He had a small birthmark over one eye, and although it was never mentioned, he was, I think, very conscious of this.

I had to confess that I had never danced (that is to say ballroom danced) in my life. It seemed that Percy had some experience in these matters and said that he would teach me.

"In fact," he said, "you really only have to walk round and skip at the corners."

A long dance dress had to be acquired for the event; the dress chosen was a creation in deep cerise pink and somewhat Spanish style that suited me very well. Demurely puff-sleeved, it was fairly fitting to the knees, where it flounced out in layers of frills.

After that first dance Percy and I went out quite a lot and became good if not romantically-inclined friends. Our dancing improved, and we soon progressed from marching round the room and skipping at the corners. The dance tunes of the times were romantic and haunting. At least that is how they seemed to me. Today they would be considered over-sentimental and sloppy, but we found them lovely to dance to. "Who's Taking You Home Tonight", "Deep Purple", "Music Maestro Please", and "The Girl in the Alice Blue Gown", to name a few which come immediately to mind.

Percy was one of the first to volunteer when the war started in 1939. Within a day or two he had joined the

RASC and departed for service. We continued to correspond and I think I am right in saying that Percy would have welcomed a relationship on a more permanent footing.

Another boyfriend acquired at Bowmakers was a very handsome lad named Ray Witt. He looked exactly like the film star Richard Greene, who in far-off days played the lead in the *Robin Hood* series. One slight snag was that he was no taller than me. We were both very aware of this, but we went about together for some months and enjoyed each other's company. At the beginning of our friendship he wrote a little poem for me.

G wen has her picture in my heart,
W hereon she looks divine.
E ven when we are far apart,
N o one can take that picture of mine.

A ll day as I work, my thoughts are of you,
R omancing as with an angel from the skies,
N {Just cannot remember this line}
O nly a dream that never dies.
L ady all a man's wishes could come true,
D eep in those beautiful eyes.

As will be seen, the first letters of each line spell my name. I was impressed. Ray and I lived at opposite ends of the town, which was a real disadvantage. Normally after our evenings out together, he saw me on my bus to Moordown and then caught his bus to

Southbourne. One evening however I missed my last bus, and was not at all keen to walk the three miles home alone. Ray was nothing if not chivalrous and agreed to walk with me. This took some time and it must have been well after midnight when we reached Evelyn Road. Poor Ray then had to get himself home. We were both only sixteen or seventeen and our mothers not used to their children arriving home later than 10.30 or 11 o'clock.

When we arrived at Evelyn Road the house was in darkness and Peggy and Mother already in bed. We decided that Ray should borrow my bicycle. Now my bicycle and Peggy's were kept overnight in the scullery, one placed against the kitchen range and the other leaning against the first. I knew that the scullery was usually left in a fairly untidy state and I did not want my boyfriend to see the chaos. Of course my bike proved to be the most difficult one to reach, and as I was determined not to switch on the light, a fairly difficult operation had to be carried out, swinging bicycles round in a very small space and in complete darkness.

Finally, our goal was achieved and Ray sped off on his five-mile ride through the black moonless night. In those days all the gas street lights were extinguished at about eleven o'clock, and anyone cycling through the night would be thought to be on some nefarious mission.

A policeman stopped poor Ray and questioned him; the embarrassment was increased when the policeman noticed a silk stocking entwined round the back spokes of the bicycle. (We often hung stockings in the scullery to dry, and no doubt in all our blundering and fumbling, the offending article had dropped on to the bicycle.) Today, I am sure that there are plenty of young people wandering the streets of Bournemouth in the early hours, but in the 1930s all the respectable young people were off the streets long before the midnight hour.

Many years later we lived near Ray and his wife for a while, and our children attended the same school. We laughed together about the incident of the stocking-draped bicycle.

CHAPTER
TEN

The War
Brings Changes

I had been enjoying my work and the social life at Bowmakers for about two years when the war came upon us in 1939. I remember cycling through the town a day or two before the declaration, when the blackout regulations were already in force and the atmosphere unspeakably eerie. It was late evening but the vehicles and bicycles carried no lights whatsoever. Shadowy traffic moved slowly and dangerously in the blackness. Normally, lights would have been streaming from shops, houses and friendly street lamps, and the headlights of cars and buses would have added to the illumination of the bustling streets as workers and shoppers made their way home. But on Friday 1st September 1939, phantom vehicles glided through the town as the apprehensive population hastened homewards.

But at first the war was a non-event. We busied ourselves making curtains of black casement and fixing black paper on wooden frames to slot over the windows. Some people stuck miles and miles of criss-crossed paper strips over their windows, because we were told that this would stop the glass splintering. The lattice effect, if carefully carried out, was not unpleasing, until the time came to clean the windows, when a choice had to be made between removing the paper and leaving the windows dirty. Mounds of sandbags appeared all over the place and notices directed the public to the nearest air raid shelters.

Some young people volunteered immediately, Percy Claxton for one, while older people enlisted as air raid wardens and firewatchers. The LDV (Local Defence Volunteers — later to be renamed the Home Guard) was formed. We all carried little cardboard boxes containing our gas masks. Plans were made to evacuate children from "danger" areas to "safe" areas. In Bournemouth we were canvassed as to how many extra beds each house could provide.

The Ministry of Food and the Fire Service began to recruit extra staff and suddenly we were all very busy getting ready for war; but fortunately, for quite a time it continued to be a "phoney" war; no bombs and apart from one false alarm on September 3rd, no air raid warnings; in fact nothing at all.

The effect of hostilities on the business of Bowmakers was very marked. They were a finance company providing money for the purchase of cars, aeroplanes, wireless sets and a hundred and one other luxuries. The war straightaway put a stop to all that and no new business came along. The existing cases continued to send their monthly instalments, but the work shrank rapidly because as accounts were completed no new ones replaced them.

A year or so before the onset of war, Bowmaker had commenced changing from the Burroughs accounting machine method of bookkeeping, to what must have been one of the first computer systems. Named the Hollerith system, it amassed information on punched cards, then fed, sorted and computed the details on giant machines. As a fairly junior member of the machine room, I was trained to be a punch card operator. Not a very interesting job, but acceptable because I was interested in the main machinery and hopeful of becoming a senior member of the staff in due course. The changeover took about a year to complete and for many months the two systems ran concurrently.

All through this period there was heaps of overtime to be worked and as we were paid a shilling per hour for evening work and 2/6 per hour for weekend work, and as I was earning only 17/6 per week at that time, I often doubled my earnings by working overtime. My mother allowed me to keep all the extra money and for the first time in my life I was able to open a post office account, and I also vastly improved my wardrobe.

But with the start of war, the work became less and less. To some extent the departure of the men and boys into the armed forces compensated for the dwindling work but as 1940 progressed, those of us who were left began to feel unsure of continued employment. Once again I was in the market for a new job.

Peggy was eighteen and a half when the war commenced. From the age of sixteen she had been very friendly with a lad named Bill Carter, whom she had met at the Baptist Church Bible Class. They were made for each other, eventually married, and had a wonderfully happy life together until, sadly, they were parted by Peggy's death in 1976.

In 1940 Bill was working for the Bournemouth Gas & Water Company, an establishment then taking on temporary clerks to replace those who had left to join up. At Bill's suggestion, I wrote the company asking if they would consider me for one of the temporary positions. I was duly interviewed and eventually started work as a cost clerk.

The work was interesting. As the title implied, the cost of running the various plants had to be ascertained. I kept the books for the Poole and Pitwines gas-making plants, and had to collect together details of the labour and materials used in making gas and its by-products. In due course all the totals for a given period were collated and priced out in relation to each thousand feet of gas made. Thus, my enthusiasm for figures and calculations was brought into use at last.

In order to do the job with reasonable efficiency, it was necessary to understand how the various plants worked. Having a liking for things logical I became very interested and absorbed all I was told by Mr Peters and Mr Moore, two of the senior cost clerks.

Even at this early stage of the war the staff of the cost office was an elderly bunch.

In charge was Mr Lyle. Thin, dapper, unsmiling and around sixty years of age, he sat at a large desk facing the rest of us and did not fraternise with the staff. I was in awe of Mr Lyle. From time to time, when he wanted the attention of a certain Ken Hayward, a young married man in his thirties who sat immediately in front of him, he snarled, "'Ayward!"

Red faced, 'Ayward would leap to Mr Lyle's side. The question always seemed to be the same.

"What's the coke stock figure at Bourne Valley, 'Ayward?"

However poor 'Ayward answered, it never seemed to please Mr Lyle, who responded with scowls and mutterings.

Apart from reigning over the costs office, Mr Lyle was also in charge of the "Sick and Burial Society" and he took this work very seriously indeed. As far as we could tell the work consisted of totalling up the fivepenny contributions made by society members each week. We could never understand why Mr Lyle did not count up the number of participating workers, and then multiply the total by five pence. His method, as borne out by his mutterings, was to add 5d and 5d to make 10d, then another 5d to make 1/3, followed by another 5d to reach 1/8 and so on.

Each evening Mr Lyle collected his trilby hat and umbrella, and prepared to leave a few minutes before the rest of us. His last task was to lock the Sick and Burial Society books in a big safe — an operation which he carried out very carefully and then headed for the door. Every evening, without fail, on reaching the door he turned round, walked back to the safe and checked that it was locked. No wartime secret was guarded more carefully than the Sick and Burial Society fivepences.

Mr Lyle must have been born in about 1880, and the story went that his parents had paid 2d a week for his schooling. A member of the staff once remarked that his parents had been "done".

Then there was Mr Fred Peters who really ran the department. He was a poppet if there ever was one. About forty-five years of age he was no beauty, having a plump red face and a long, some time broken, hooked nose. But he was kind, helpful to everyone and shouldered all the responsibilities of the office.

In the corner sat Mr Henry Moore, a tiny old man of well over sixty years. Mr Moore was reputed to be very clever and we understood that in the past he had held high office in the company. A story prevailed that Mr Moore had "fixed the books" in some way, but did it so cleverly that no one had been able to unravel the figures. Eventually, the auditors had to beg Henry to show them how the "cooking" had been done, and in return, the company agreed to retain his services, although in a comparatively lowly position.

Henry was a law unto himself and cared for no one. He ignored Mr Lyle most of the time and certainly was not afraid of him; if the need arose, Henry would shout and snarl at Mr Lyle and give as good as he got. He often walked into the office ten minutes late, having depended on hitching a lift to travel from his home in Poole; no one dared to criticise. No doubt, when his big misdeed was sorted out he had been guaranteed a job for life. Petty indiscretions could not harm Henry.

Henry was a rose grower and throughout the rose season arrived at the office with a bloom in his buttonhole. By the end of the day, the rose, by the natural order of things, had wilted, but as Henry left the office, he handed the drooping flower to one of the female members of the staff with some ceremony. You could not help liking the old rogue, although he had some very off-putting habits.

I suppose Miss Madge was the senior lady clerk. She was, I suspect, in her early forties, very prim and extremely efficient. She sat in the front row of the middle block of desks, and had a board arranged across the open front of the kneehole desk. Whether this was to protect her legs from draughts or to shield them from the prying eyes of the lads in the next door wages office, I did not discover.

Then there was Miss Hopkins, a tall, pleasant girl of about twenty-seven years. Mavis was engaged to a soldier fighting for us all in the Middle East, and her conversation was largely limited to whether she had received a letter from Norman and the state of her kidneys. To alleviate a minor kidney problem, she had been told to drink X gallons of water each day. Poor Mavis had bottles of the stuff lined up on her desk, and steadily drank her way through them. Not surprisingly, she had to pop out of the office every half hour or so.

The office boy, a good-looking lad of sixteen, had an unfortunate speech impediment, which meant that he could not use the telephone. As I was the next most junior member of the staff, I was constantly at Mr Lyle's beck and call. "Miss Arnold' get Mr So and So on the telephone for me, will you," was his everlasting cry. I didn't mind jumping up and down all day, but did sometimes wonder why he could not get a few numbers himself, since his main occupation was just adding fivepences.

Two other ladies completed the staff. They were not members of the costing team, but in charge of the company co-partnership scheme. Both were unbelievably old-fashioned. Either would have fitted well into a pre-First World War office. Miss Steel, the senior of the two, was I would say about fifty-eight. Short, plump, with a birdlike smiling face, she lived with her sister, and when she indulged in small talk, which was not very often, her remarks always started "My sister said . . ."

Miss Steel's assistant, Miss Kennedy, might have been any age between twenty-two and fifty-five. She was so shy, demure and old-fashioned that she never ever spoke a word, unless in reply to some query regarding her work. Then it would just be "Yes, Miss Steel" or "No, Miss Steel". At such a great effort she would lower her eyes and blush profusely. Both these ladies wore very old-fashioned, nondescript clothes and appeared to live in quiet little worlds of their own.

The wages office next door was connected to the cost office by a glass hatch window. The wages team had been all male, but when I arrived on the scene only two or three young men were still in residence. There was always a certain amount of larking about going on in the wages office, which Mr Lyle, who sat with his back towards the hatch, could not see. I could see. They always seemed to be having great fun. At a much later date I was told that great interest was taken in the bobbing up and down to the telephone that I was obliged to do. I also learned that they were glad I had not followed Miss Madge's example by fixing a piece of board across the front of my desk. I was completely unaware of their interest in my anatomy!

Soon after I joined the Bournemouth Gas & Water Company, one of the wages office boys left to join the army. I did not know him at all. Our total conversation was limited to an occasional "Good morning". This particular boy was tall, fair, blue-eyed and by any standard, handsome, but he was also exceedingly shy. His mother worked for the company and she made it her business to get to know me. A pleasant talkative little lady, she constantly waylaid me and quite soon I knew a considerable amount about her family and I'm sure she gathered details of mine. After John left to join the army, she asked me if I would write to him. I said I would, if he wrote to me in the first place, and a correspondence started which was to have a considerable effect on my life in the years to come.

So I continued to work in the cost office. I liked the work, the hours were short by the standards of the day, and over two and a half years my wage slowly increased to 22 shillings and sixpence per week.

CHAPTER
ELEVEN

Dunkirk, the Long Winter of 1940 and Beyond

I suppose it was Dunkirk that first made the war real for us. The wireless news reported the progress or rather the lack of progress, of our forces in Europe, but somehow it all seemed far away and I suppose we got almost used to the bulletins. News of retreat reached us and then suddenly the town was full of war-weary soldiers.

Troops of many nationalities and colours filled the streets. I suppose I had only seen one or two black people in my life, for they were an absolute rarity in those days. There were also Belgian, French and many British soldiers. All were dressed in tattered remains of uniforms and all looked gaunt and dirty. Accommodation was quickly found for them in local schools, but during the day, the war-weary men just filled the town.

I remember seeing bedraggled soldiers pressed against local girls on street corners. I really could not understand that sort of behaviour. I only knew about occasional goodnight kisses and an arm slid gently round the waist. Sometime afterwards a number of fatherless babies appeared, many of them coloured.

I have a clear recollection of an enormous black soldier knocking at our front door. We were terrified, but he only requested a drink of water and followed Mother through to the kitchen, drank the water and left, leaving us quaking with fear.

After a few weeks the men were rekitted and sent to various units, leaving life in gentle old Bournemouth to return to normal.

Soon after Dunkirk, the Battle of Britain commenced and daily bulletins reported our Air Force's successes. In Bournemouth we were, I think, just a little too far west to see much of the action.

Social life continued with little interruption. My weekends were spent with Irene visiting either the theatre, the "pictures" or dancing. All the local lads were away at the war. Casual boyfriends came and went but we had no special allegiance to any of them; we were free to befriend any of the many servicemen posted to Bournemouth. We were never short of dancing partners and we both became good and enthusiastic dancers.

At home we adjusted to the wartime inconveniences of rationing, blackouts and air raids. The last named imposed a great strain during the winter of 40/41 because although Bournemouth was not a target area, it did seem to be on the route to everywhere. I now realise that the planes flew in on radio beams, and found their targets by reference to intersecting beams.

No doubt this accounted for the fact that night after night, enemy planes droned in single file over the town. During the first half of every night, a continuous procession of aircraft flew in; throughout the second half of the night, still in single file, they flew out again. Each night the planes made for specific cities: Coventry, Cardiff, Birmingham, Liverpool, Plymouth, Southampton, Portsmouth, not to mention London itself and many others. Quite obviously, the people living in the target areas suffered far more than we did. We knew that we were not the target, but we were kept in states of nervous tension every night during the whole of that winter, because the planes had a nasty habit of dropping the occasional bomb. It seemed that on their homeward flights, realising that a bomb was left on board, they dropped it on Bournemouth rather than "waste" it by letting it go over the sea.

So it was that throughout that long winter the dreaded siren sounded at dusk every night, and the "All-Clear" was not heard until three, four, five or even six o'clock the next morning. Mother, Peggy and I crouched in the tiny cupboard under the stairs all those hours. We sat on boxes with only a candle to lighten the gloom. It was the worst period of the war for me. For hour after hour we listened to the distinctive throb of the German bombers (we could always tell if it was "one of ours" or "one of theirs"), the gunfire and an occasional earth-shattering explosion. At times I physically shook with fear. It was not so much fear of harm to our persons, but fear of losing our home. Home meant everything to us and I could not imagine how we would ever make another home, if we lost the house and our possessions. We knew nothing of house or house contents insurance. To me our modest little dwelling was irreplaceable and it was threatened every night. Strangely, when later in the war I sat under a legitimate target, I felt little fear.

I have never longed so much for the arrival of lighter evenings than I did that winter. As the days grew longer, so the air raid warnings came a little later each evening, and there was time for more normal living before we crawled into the cupboard under the stairs. As 1940 gave way to 1941, I knew exactly how many minutes of extra daylight each new day would bring. Darkness meant terror; daylight meant rest and relief. I felt that I would never grumble about anything again, once the day arrived when we could climb into our beds and fall asleep without fear. Even now, so many years later, as I settle down to sleep, I often think of that winter and thank God for nights of peace.

Our days were more or less normal; we continued to work, and somehow dealt with the weariness which we must have felt. Some people had Anderson shelters erected in their gardens or Morrison table shelters in their houses; in either case they could at least lie down and get some rest between explosions. I do not remember why we did not have a proper shelter. Perhaps as Bournemouth was not a target area, shelters were not provided. If it was a matter of purchasing your own, we would surely not have been able to afford to buy.

Even so, as a family our finances were improving and we now paid Gan-Gan rent for the house. Both Peggy and I had wage increases from time to time, but we still passed the bulk of our earnings to Mother. We also managed to save for home improvements. Jointly, we put away half a crown (2/6 or 12½p), towards the purchase of a gas geyser for the bathroom. No more hauling buckets of boiling water up the stairs, no more using half a hundredweight of coal to get the kitchen range going. But the simple luxury of being able to enjoy a bath at any time was marred during the bombing winter by the fear of a raid developing while partaking of the pleasure. We were so excessively modest in those days, that the fear of finding one self tipped into the street in the nude was every bit as great as the fear of injury.

One story which seemed particularly horrifying to me, was of a local lady whose house was bombed whilst she was taking a bath. She ended up in the front garden with the bath upside-down on top of her. The bath had in fact saved her life by protecting her from most of the falling masonry. That part of the story did not impress me; all I could consider was how devastated she must have felt, when the rescuing firemen lifted the bath off of her revealing her nakedness!

Another example of my primness was that I worried quite a bit about the possibility of being rescued with hairpins or curlers in place. Like most girls who affected the longish wavy hairstyle of the day, I pinned up the "ends" of my hair at night. It would have embarrassed me greatly to be caught with hairpins in place. When the siren sounded, as soon as I had taken my place in the cupboard under the stairs, all my hairpins were removed and placed in my pocket. When the "All-Clear" blew, all the hairpins had to be replaced. This routine became such a habit, that years after the raids ended, I often awoke to find my hairpins in my pyjamas pocket or under my pillow, the result of dreaming that an air raid was taking place.

At this time Peggy worked as a counter assistant for Malmesbury & Parsons Dairies. It was considered a "nice" job, only superior girls were employed and I think Peggy was happy there. At some stage during her adolescence, she ceased to attend the Congregational Sunday School, and became involved with the Winton Baptist Church. I too joined their Bible Class but never became quite as active as Peggy. It was at the Baptist Church that Peggy met Bill Carter and from there their romance flourished. I think she was sixteen and Bill seventeen when they started "walking out". They regularly had two evenings a week at the "pictures", and on Saturdays Bill met Peggy from work and they meandered home together. Sunday afternoons and evenings found them at church. They never seemed to tire of each other's company and to the best of my knowledge, neither ever showed interest in the company of other boys or girls. Bill was a most kindhearted and generous man and they were in every way a perfect pair.

When the war came, Bill volunteered for the Air Force and trained to be a navigator. I have a picture of him in my mind now, tall, thin and slightly stooping, with his forage cap bearing its white flash perched on his crinkly fair hair.

On 6th June 1942, under a flawless blue sky Peggy and Bill were married. I was the only bridesmaid and Uncle Reg (Arnold) gave the bride away. The reception took place at home and was a very happy occasion. After they had left for their honeymoon in Lynton, I recall that a violent thunderstorm raged. But there was nothing prophetic about that for there was never a happier couple.

In those early days there was no question of Peggy and Bill having a home of their own. In common with most wartime young couples they had to make their base with parents. Now for the first time we did not have a lodger in the big front bedroom; the room became Peggy and Bill's room.

As a Navigator/Sgt Bill's pay was good, and by the time he came home on his first leave, enough money had been saved to equip the room with a carpet and a bed. In the way one remembers isolated incidents, I have a clear recollection of Bill walking into that bedroom for the first time, and viewing with obvious satisfaction the newly acquired bed and carpet. He then walked round hanging his clothes on imaginary hooks, and putting things away into imaginary drawers. Peggy and I thought it was very funny.

Bill completed his Air Force training and made one or two operational flights, before becoming very ill with pneumonia. On the first flight after Bill had been taken into hospital, his plane and its crew failed to return. After the illness the Medical Officer decided that Bill was not A1 and was unfit for flying duties. Eventually he transferred to the Army and completed his war service as an army surveyor.

Peggy also had a narrow escape. She had been directed into munitions work, and was called upon to do very tough shift work in an armaments factory in Westover Road, Bournemouth. On leaving the factory one Sunday lunchtime in May 1943, she planned to "window shop" at Beales the large departmental store nearby. She was looking for a handbag, which was to be a 21st birthday present for me. The girl who usually cycled home with Peggy was late leaving the factory, and Peggy felt peeved to be kept waiting. But while she waited, a huge landmine demolished Beales' six-storey building 150 yards from where she stood. She was very shocked and shaken, but not physically harmed. But for the delay while she waited for her colleague, Peggy would have been gazing in Beales' shop window at the very moment the explosion happened.

Peggy and Bill continued to make Evelyn Road their home, and both their sons were born before they had a home of their own. Robert John arrived on 21st May 1944 and Alan David on 5th July 1948. Alan was born on the first day of the new National Health scheme when various benefits became available for the first time. I well remember how Peggy hoped that Alan would not arrive before the fifth. He was born in the small hours of the appointed day.

For me 1942 signalled the end of a chapter of my life. All single girls had to register and were liable to be called up for essential war service on reaching the age of twenty. This could be a branch of the armed services, that is to say the ATS, WAAF or the WRENS. The other options were the Fire Service, the Land Army, Nursing or Munitions work. As I was employed by a Public Utility company, I could most probably have claimed exemption from call-up, but as my 20th birthday drew near, I decided that the time had come to spread my wings and leave my very sheltered life at home.

CHAPTER TWELVE

The Big Adventure Starts

Today was different, although in many ways it was a very ordinary day. It was raining, which was usual enough. I was late, and that was not remarkable. I knew that by pedalling hard, I could cover the three miles to the office in time to sign in above the red line.

My thoughts were not on work as I joined dozens of other cyclists all heading towards the town and mostly wearing yellow rain capes identical to mine. My thoughts were centred on the contents of a letter newly arrived that morning.

I freewheeled down the long hill of Dean Park Road, across the main Old Christchurch Road and came to a halt behind the offices of the Bournemouth Gas & Water Company. Bike held high, I clattered down the iron stairs to the bicycle sheds and then sprinted into the cloakroom reserved for the female staff.

In the cloakroom a few other girls who would have to fly to sign on before nine o'clock wrestled with their raincoats and patted their dripping locks into some sort of order before dashing towards the lift.

The clerk whose job it was to rule the line at nine o'clock stood by the signing-in book tapping his ruler and eyeing the clock. I signed in the very nick of time and raced on towards the Costs office.

My colleagues were already seated, with ledgers on desks and pens poised if not actually in motion. Polite, but slightly chilly "Good Mornings" drifted towards me, but for once the disapproving glances did not put me in my place.

"Morning, morning — I've got my papers!"

I ripped the newly arrived letter from my handbag and held it aloft. The group of elderly gentlemen and primly mature ladies stopped work with one accord, and focused their attention on me.

"Tuesday 26th January I have to report to RAF Innsworth. That gives me just a fortnight, Mr Peters."

Mr Peters, the office manager, was a plump, genial man in his fifties. His spaniel eyes betrayed a mild disposition that contrasted strangely with his large and very crooked nose. He muttered something about the replacement not being nearly ready, but smiled and said kindly, "The big adventure starts then, Miss Arnold."

The others, after a few dutiful "Well, wells", returned to their ledgers. They had heard it all before.

I hauled my work on to my desk and stared at it; but BTUs, therms and the cost of running a gas-making plant meant little to me that day.

I had volunteered. Although, I must confess, with the knowledge that I was in any case likely to be called up within months; twenty was the critical age for girls. My sister Peggy had been directed into munitions work when she became twenty, but she had been allowed to work near home. Mother was a widow and in such cases, one daughter was permitted to work locally for the mother's comfort. When I became twenty, I too might have obtained deferment on the grounds that I worked in an essential industry, but I was keen to go.

After twenty years of very sheltered existence I was ready to branch out. Excepting a weekend Girl Guide camp, two holidays staying with my uncle in Basingstoke and a week imposing on a school friend's aunt in Staines, every night of my twenty years had been spent in the house where I had been born. I was keen to join the ranks of those serving King and Country. Keen, but apprehensive. "The war could last for years," they said, but without a doubt I was eager to go.

Enquiries had revealed that girls were needed in the ATS and in the WAAF. A pity, I had fancied joining the WRENS. True to form I made the final decision for an inconsequential reason; I decided that it should be the WAAF because although not as smart as the navy blue of the WRENS, air force blue would be more flattering than khaki.

After completing the initial forms at the local Labour Exchange, there had arrived instructions and a railway warrant to attend the recruiting office in Southampton.

We travelled so little in those days that just making the 30-mile journey to bomb-scarred Southampton was an adventure. There, after a medical examination which seemed designed to shock the modest little innocent that I was, and more form filling, I was soon on my way home with the knowledge that I was A1 and would shortly be told when and where to present myself.

So now my papers had arrived. It had happened to so many of my acquaintances and now it was my turn.

"Report to RAF Innsworth 26.1.43." Again a railway warrant was provided, together with details of the route, down to the precise train I was to board at Bournemouth West station. Bring a small suitcase, the instructions said, pyjamas, toilet requisites, a large sheet of brown paper, some string and be sure to wear strong shoes. What on earth was the paper and string for?

It is hard to believe now that we did not possess a small suitcase, or that acquiring one presented a problem. In my circles, money was seldom spent on unnecessary articles. The required case was eventually obtained, given to me by a kindly old lady who ran the local sweetshop. The very cardboardy case had been presented to her by a confectionery salesman, as a reward for orders placed. It was tidy and it filled my need. (It has in fact proved to be almost indestructible; all these years later I still use it to store Christmas decorations.)

My "toilet requisites" included three tablets of Imperial Leather soap. A present from a well-wisher which did not do Cussons, the makers, any favour; I've loathed Imperial Leather soap ever since because it still brings to my mind memories of those first Spartan WAAF days.

The 26th arrived, as all days do. My staid, but generous colleagues at the Bournemouth Gas & Water Company presented me with a fountain pen and a poem of kind thoughts:

Sonnet to Gwen

We hope that you'll accept this, Gwen,
Our token of affection;
And when you use this fountain pen
'Twill waken recollection
Of happy days in office life,
Which now for you have ended;
You too are joining in the strife,
With charm and courage blended.
We hope your path will prove as sweet
As once it was in Civvie Street.

I said my "goodbyes" at home and set off for Bournemouth West station alone. The world in general, and the war in particular, awaited me.

CHAPTER
THIRTEEN

ACW2 Arnold
476735

I remember my "going away" outfit very clearly. Best camel coat, brown velvet beret, brown suede shoes and a warm dress which had been designed and made in a soft shade of pink by the local dressmaker.

On the train I met another recruit, a woman of the world four or five years older than me and very sophisticated. We made an ill-matched couple, but as people who have been thrown together by circumstance do, we chatted throughout the journey, each trying to calm her jangling nerves on the other.

When we finally alighted at Gloucester station, two or three dozen young women, all clutching small suitcases and wearing strong shoes, emerged from the train. We were herded towards a large RAF transport and for the first of many hundred times, I clambered with a marked lack of agility, into the back of a service transport vehicle.

I cannot remember the exact sequence of events on our arrival at the camp, but can say that at an early stage we were allocated to huts, each equipped to sleep

48 girls. Adjacent were ablution huts that contained rows of lavatories and washbasins. The cookhouse, which was some three or four hundred yards from the sleeping quarters, was found and the fare sampled. Finally, late in the evening, we were taken to the NAAFI and told that our time was our own until the Tannoy sounded next morning.

Forty-eight oddly assorted strangers settled down for their first night in His Majesty's Air Force. Not only the "long and the short and the tall", we had the "posh and the common", the "tearful and the giggly", the "I feel sick", the "chatterboxes", the "know-alls" and the "where are the men?". What a job lot! Incidentally, the "where are the men?" group were right out of luck; Innsworth was populated by thousands of females and about half a dozen men.

Forty-eight small iron bedsteads were provided, and the corporal in charge introduced us to our "biscuits". (For the uninitiated, a forces' mattress consisted of three small mattresses, each about two feet by two feet, and known as "biscuits".)

The Innsworth "biscuits" were harder and more awful than any encountered later. The pillows were stuffed with straw, pieces of which penetrated the outer covers in a tormenting fashion. The blankets weighed a ton. But we had had a long and exciting day, and we were young.

We slept.

CHAPTER
FOURTEEN

MT Driver, Batwoman or RDF Operator?

January 27th soon arrived. The Tannoy sounded I think at 7am, and in accordance with instructions we rose to wash in the unfamiliar and very public conditions of the ablutions hut; we then dressed as circumspectly as possible and at the corporal's bidding "stacked" our bedding.

The moon was still shining as we made our way along the puddled paths to the cookhouse. What on earth was I doing? Why had I volunteered? Yesterday I had breakfasted in our cosy kitchen at home; today I had arisen from a straw-stuffed pillow, and waded through mud by the light of a watery moon to eat in a huge hangar built to accommodate several thousand people.

The war might already be three years old, but there was every possibility that it would go on for ever. I was "in", this was "it". Oh, Gwen!

The next few days were busy. Instructions were showered on us at every turn. We could write home, but we had no address.

"Tell your parents that you can't receive letters here." We were staying only six or seven days and there were no facilities for incoming mail. Oh dear, I knew Peggy would be waiting, pen in hand, to get a letter to me. The fact that I had left home only yesterday did not mean that I was not longing for news.

We were herded from hut to hut for various formalities. Intelligence tests, more forms, more medicals — less and less modesty. How could girls be so varied in shape and so generally odd looking when undressed? Still more forms to fill in, more instructions and of course an introduction to "square bashing".

One important matter to be decided was the trade in which the recruit would be employed, for however long the war was to last. Before I left home, my mother had made me promise that I would not become an MT driver. She had found my joining up very hard to accept, and had forcibly pointed out that she simply could not face life if she had to think of me driving a lorry up and down the country, so I had promised that, come what may, I would not become an MT driver.

When the trade allocation hut was reached, we found that only three trades were open to us. We all had to be slotted into one of these three trades. We all had to be MT drivers, batwomen or RDF operators.

MT driving was out and I was appalled at the thought of spending the rest of the war as a batwoman. Since leaving school I had progressed up the social scale from shoe shop assistant to filing clerk, thence to punch card operator and finally to cost clerk. Was I now to become a batwoman? Just a servant? Oh, the humiliation and the sheer boredom of it! If only I could make RDF operator. I entered this on the form as my first choice.

The literature provided at the Southampton interview had mentioned RDF operating, and that it was a Grade 2 trade requiring a good educational standard and a sound knowledge of geometry. Now my education had given geometry very little attention. From the start, I had liked the sound of Radio Direction Finding, and during the weeks before my call-up I had the foresight to borrow a book on elementary geometry from the public library. I think I spent a couple of hours on my study, memorising a few terms but little else. Would my sketchy knowledge enable me to bluff my way into the only acceptable trade?

I shall never forget the anguish of that particular Innsworth session, when I was resident in the trade allocation hut for more than an entire day. Nearly every girl in my squad was called to interview before me. Would I ever know my fate? At long last my name was called, and I sat before the officer who was empowered to decide how I would spend the next three and a half years.

I was asked half a dozen general geometry questions. I got one or two of them wrong and lied, "I haven't thought about the subject since I left school — I'm sure it will all come back to me."

I did not mention that no one had required me to think very much about the subject, either at school or since. I very much wanted to become an RDF operator and was prepared to tell white lies.

"Well, Arnold," the interviewer said at last, "you did exceptionally well in the intelligence tests. I think you are suitable for RDF training."

Oh, the relief! My prayers were answered.

"Kitting out" provided an interesting day at Innsworth. Everyone who has been in the forces has, no doubt, had much the same experience. We were marched into a huge hangar, and on entering handed kitbags. Recruits then moved from counter to counter, as items of kit were thrown into the bag. Size was considered only vaguely. Generally speaking, the garments increased in length and width at the same rate. It will be realised that those who were tall and thin or short and fat, had problems.

Two skirts, two jackets, one greatcoat, one hat, three shirts, six collars, one tie, one grey cardigan, two bras, two pairs of corselets, three pairs of winter "passion killers" (black), three pairs of summer ditto (grey Celanese), two vests, three pairs of thick grey stockings, two pairs of flat black laced shoes and two sets of mannish striped pyjamas. Various oddments, the usefulness of which was not apparent at the time, included a button stick, white cotton belt of strange design with numerous tabs and tapes attached and a calico ration bag. A "tin" hat, gas mask, and a ground sheet that doubled as a Mac, completed the goodies. When this amazing collection of wearing apparel was deposited higgledy-piggledy in my kitbag, I certainly could not lift it (and never could for that matter). The bag had to be dragged back to the hut.

Back in the sleeping quarters we were told to change into our newly acquired uniforms. If the scene could have been filmed, I suspect that it would have been hilariously funny. Nothing fitted, we had no mirrors, no one knew how to tie a tie, and all the unsuitable hair styles had somehow to be controlled and got "off the collar". If we were an ill-assorted lot before acquiring our uniforms, now, having dressed up, we all had at least one thing in common. We all looked equally ill at ease and awful.

"Now," said the corporal, "make a parcel of your civilian clothes, address it to your home and fall in outside the hut in ten minutes."

So this was what the brown paper and string was for. We struggled inexpertly to organise the last symbols of civilian life into passable looking parcels. Then, clutching our strangely shaped and inefficiently packed bundles, we "fell in" outside the hut.

We set off to march to the camp post office. I must mention that it was raining, as it did every day during our stay at Innsworth. Not a gentle shower of rain, but great sheets of driving rain. The distance from the hut to the post office, including an exposed 800 yards around the huge parade ground, was about a mile. There was no shelter from the driving rain. Dressed in our unfamiliar new uniforms, topped by our wet-weather gear (rectangular groundsheet with a hole in the middle for the wearer's head), and clutching our brown paper parcels, the motley squad strode bravely towards the post office. Being 5 feet 7 inches tall, I found myself in the front line of the squad, marching into the merciless rain without the protection of a girl in front of me, and with my groundsheet flapping uselessly away from me. My parcel and I were both soaked through and through.

When we arrived at the post office, the sodden piece of brown paper had given up the task imposed upon it, and sad little bits of civilian clothing edged through in many places.

"Quite unacceptable," declared the post office clerk.

I had to agree that my parcel was not fit to make the journey to Bournemouth.

Back to the sleeping quarters marched the squad, one or two of us still hugging bundles, and respectable sheets of brown paper provided by the kindly post office woman. The rest of the squad was then free until teatime. ACW2 Arnold and another victim of being in the front line of the squad repacked their parcels and faced the elements once more.

Some years later, my mother told me how upset she had been to receive the pathetic parcel of damp crumpled clothes. Now as a mother and grandmother myself I can understand how she felt. The end of an era had arrived and no doubt she felt a great wave of sadness.

CHAPTER
FIFTEEN

Innsworth
and a Journey

One afternoon, perhaps it was at the weekend, having some free time I agreed to accompany another girl to the only public phone box on the camp. There we joined a queue of recruits all waiting to telephone home. We watched as each girl entered the box, lifted the receiver, inserted her two pennies, waited, pressed button "A" and then her lips formed the words "Hello Mum".

Every girl then dissolved into tears, squandering part of the precious three minutes. I can imagine how depressing this was for the Mums, waiting at the end of the line for reassuring news. I thought the little pantomime quite funny at the time; we did not have a telephone at home, so I was but a spectator.

Innsworth was a huge camp filled with rows and rows of huts. It was all too easy to lose your bearings, simply because there were so few landmarks. Every row of huts looked just like every other row of huts.

One night I decided to make use of the bath hut which was situated some distance from our sleeping quarters. I set out carrying pyjamas and toilet equipment, and found the hut without difficulty.

The tiny wooden building was partitioned into two bathrooms, each about six foot by seven foot. Illumination of the entire area depended on one small blue light bulb strategically placed above the central partition. There was to be no risk of helping a stray enemy bomber on its way, as the outer door opened; the light was so dim, that would-be users had to feel around to discover at which end of the bath the taps were placed. However, vision was not needed to know that the bath was very grimy. The scum and residue from countless previous bathers had left the sides of the bath rough and thoroughly unpleasant to touch.

I had been forewarned that all service baths and washbasins were plugless. I also knew that the accepted solution was a penny wrapped in a handkerchief. Unfortunately, this makeshift arrangement did not fit the aperture perfectly, making it necessary to carry out the bathing operation at speed before the water disappeared.

A bath of sorts achieved, striped pyjamas and greatcoat donned, I set out to find my way back to the sleeping quarters. Every row of huts looked exactly like the next row, and I was well and truly lost. At one time I found myself on the vast parade ground! I wandered, shivering in the cold January air, for about thirty minutes before finding my hut. It was a great relief; I had been getting a mental picture of a frozen body littering the parade ground when the first squad "fell in" next morning.

So passed our six or seven days at the reception centre.

* * *

On the day we were to leave Innsworth the Tannoy sounded very early, I think at about five o'clock. By 5.45am we were assembled for instructions and departure. But before saying goodbye to the delights and discomforts of Innsworth, we experienced our first pay parade. As all ex-members of the forces will know, this involves parading and then standing at ease until your name is called.

"Arnold."

"SIR! 735." (last three numbers of 476735).

Then come smartly to attention, quick march to the paying officer's table and a crisp salute, before scooping up the goodies. On this occasion, my pay was a ten-shilling note (50 pence). Not an exciting amount, even in 1943.

Loaded with kitbags, suitcases and well-filled calico ration bags, we were then packed into transports. I have the impression that a very small number of vehicles was used to convey a very large number of recruits, from the camp to Gloucester station. The countless shuttle journeys took hours. Having a surname which started with "A", I was one of the first to arrive at the station, there to stand in an ever lengthening queue, as load after load of girls joined us.

That morning forms one of my most enduring memories of WAAF days. Imagine a dismal railway station. Outside it is still very dark and the rain sheets down relentlessly. Inside, only a minimal amount of illumination is allowed, and the atmosphere is so damp and cold that above each girl her breath hovers mistily.

Gloucester station is slowly filling with the enormous intake of recruits. Servicewomen of one week's standing, all so unaccustomed to the regimented new life, all trying to put on a good face, but all so much missing the warmth and comfort of home.

In typically British fashion, the girls start to sing. They sing and sing all the popular songs of the day. The impromptu singing is surprisingly good, clear and tuneful. When they come to "You are my sunshine" the young voices rise, taking the tune slowly and making it sound like a lament. Suddenly we all become aware of the emotion and sadness of our companions, and struggle to prevent the veil of braveness from being torn aside. I never hear "You are my sunshine" without recalling that damp February morning and seeing in my mind's eye the mass of girls on Gloucester station.

We did not know our destination, but the early start and our brimming ration bags suggested that we were to travel some way.

Liquid refreshment, we were told, would be provided from trolleys on the platforms of the stations where we were scheduled to stop. The theory of the arrangement was fine, but I found for the second time that day that it was a disadvantage to have a surname starting with "A". Not only had the "As" spent the maximum time waiting on the cheerless station, but when drinks were provided, our front carriage was always beyond the extremity of the platform. The WVS ladies could not reach us with their mugs of tea and the carriage doors were locked; the luckless "As" could only watch enviously from the carriage windows, while mugs of steaming beverage were handed to the fortunate "Bs" to "Zs".

CHAPTER
SIXTEEN

Three Weeks
at the Seaside

Our destination proved to be Morecambe. We arrived in late afternoon before daylight faded and, for once, it was not raining. Quickly and efficiently, we were sorted into squads and each squad put in the charge of a WAAF corporal.

Our group set off marching briskly along seaside roads flanked by narrow apartment houses.

A small diversion was provided by a recruit who contended that she was related to the Lupino Lane family. The mother of this little celebrity joined us at Morecambe station, and toddled along beside her daughter in a very unmilitary fashion. How she knew when and where to meet her daughter remains a mystery, but there she was, providing unintentional comic relief by maintaining a tearful conversation with her daughter as the squad marched along.

We were to be billeted in boarding houses adjacent to the seafront, so from time to time the little band was halted, while Cpl Fenn dropped off her charges in groups of eight or ten.

Each batch was given two items of information: where we were to assemble the next morning and our official address.

The boarding house I shared with nine other girls was a tremendous improvement on Innsworth. An appetising "high tea" was spread in readiness for us. My bed, though just a camp bed, was clean and comfortable. Our spirits rose.

Tea over, I hurriedly wrote a note to Mother and Peggy and just made the last post from the pillar box at the corner of the street. At last I had an address and my letter was on its way to Bournemouth. Soon my greatest need would be filled — I would have a letter from home. Although home was at the other end of the country, I was the first girl in the squad to receive a letter. No one else had rushed out that first night to post off details of our address.

The organisation at Morecambe was excellent. Not only were we quickly despatched to our billets, but we found that our boarding house landlady had given careful attention to every detail. Each day, two of the ten girls were made orderlies and were responsible for clearing the tables and washing up. In this way a five-day rota was established. On the day of duty the two orderlies were permitted to take baths and wash hair. By the standards of 1943, a bath every five days was considered adequate; we accepted the arrangement without question.

One slightly embarrassing instruction at my billet was that "certain personal articles were to be wrapped into little parcels and dropped in the kitchen boiler".

"My old father," said the landlady, "sits by the boiler all day, but he won't take any notice of you."

In 1943 we were very shy about our bodily functions, and dropping those little "parcels" into the boiler was a real worry and embarrassment to me.

There was much to be done. Every day we were assembled by Cpl Fenn and marched from venue to venue. All the large halls in the area had been requisitioned for our use. In teeming rain, we marched up and down the promenade to five or six different locations every day. Lectures were arranged to cover every aspect of service life, from the history and organisation of the RAF, to how to "spit and polish" our black laced shoes.

The timetable for each day's activity was very tight, and journeys from site to site had to be made at speed. Drill and PE figured prominently on our agenda, and as PE involved a "striptease", we learnt to dress and undress in almost no time at all.

The ballroom of the Winter Gardens, the pride of Morecambe, was our usual PE venue. Imagine thirty or forty girls dashing into the grand ballroom, and there divesting themselves of respirator, "tin" hat, rain cape, greatcoat, hat, jacket, skirt, collar, tie, corselet, stockings and shoes in order to prance about the dance floor in their unflattering knickers and collarless shirts; all to the considerable amusement of groups of sniggering workmen who always seemed to be lurking in the background.

PE over, Cpl Fenn yelled, "Fall in outside in two minutes."

Back we swooped to our individual heaps of attire and on we threw our unfamiliar and awkward garments. Corselet, woollen stockings, laced shoes, collar, tie, skirt, jacket, greatcoat, hat, rain cape, grabbed respirators and "tin" hats and then looking like a horde of demented scarecrows, rushed out to join the squad.

Tramp, tramp, tramp on to the next venue.

There were inoculations, vaccinations, gas drills, more and more lectures and endless whizzing up and down the promenade. We knew whom we had to salute, how we had to salute, our leave and rail warrant entitlements, the ranks of the Royal Air Force and their equivalents in the Army, Navy and American forces, the rates of pay, and how after three years of "undiscovered crime" we might qualify for good conduct pay of 2 pence per day.

Our schedule always included a mid-morning coffee break. Most of the little cafes used for this purpose provided delicious home-made cakes and steaming coffee for a penny or two. They were all good, but some so exceptional that each morning brought interested speculation as to whether we would be marched to this or that favourite establishment.

After high tea in our billets we were let loose in Morecambe. On my first walk out, I caught a glimpse of myself in a shop window. Mirrors, except those of the handbag variety, had not been available to us; my reflection in the shop window was something of a shock. My greatcoat reached to within a few inches of the ground. I looked like little orphan Annie!

Although we had been told that uniforms must on no account be altered, I found a Jewish tailor who undertook to shorten the offending garment for me. A stealthy trip along the backstreets after tea to deposit the coat, and another journey two hours later to pay 5/- and collect the improved garment rectified that small matter.

Our evening entertainment was curtailed by lack of money and men. Even so, we did sometimes return to the scene of our PE activities — the Winter Gardens. The dance floor was fine, the band good enough and the surroundings lush, but the clientele almost 100% female. Like Innsworth, Morecambe had been completely taken over by the WAAF and there was little chance of finding a male partner. The handful of servicemen who frequented the Winter Gardens must have been the most pampered in Britain!

At the Winter Gardens one evening, the girl who claimed to be a relative of Lupino Lane took it upon herself to sing "Jealousy" with the orchestra. She sang very well, and for effect, lounged against one of the ballroom pillars adopting the attitude of the Hollywood stars of the day — a little incongruous in an ill-fitting WAAF uniform. Perhaps she was related to the Lupino Lane family after all!

I have no recollection of social high spots or of romantic conquests in Morecambe. The odds, in the form of a dearth of men and money, were heavily stacked against us.

Our pay at the time was two shillings a day, out of which I made an allotment of 6d per day to my mother. Even in 1943 an income of 10/6 (52½ p) per week was fairly restricting. I recall that with my first letter from home came a very welcome gift of half a crown (12½ p). At the time, as my purse contained only a few coppers, the half crown seemed great wealth. However, I foolishly announced my good fortune to my nine companions and the coin was stolen from my purse. I had never before, nor have I since, had money stolen from me.

I suspected one particular girl, a little toughie from Birmingham; I may well have been wrong. I had little in common with the girl and certainly did not consider her a close friend, yet we must have exchanged addresses, because after the war she wrote asking if she could spend a week with me in Bournemouth. However, I'm afraid I did not feel inclined to add a free holiday to the half crown.

Our spell in Morecambe lasted three weeks, making our total service up to one month. We were beginning to look less raw. Hair was controlled and more or less off our collars, ties were reasonably tied, and shoes and buttons showed the beginnings of a shine. Our marching was improving despite arms that ached from the numerous injections and inoculations. We were in good heart and homesickness was receding. No doubt the wholesome food, the comfort of our billets and the kindness of the landladies helped a great deal.

Then the day arrived when we were assembled in a theatre to be given our posting instructions. This event was not well planned. Officers seated on the stage read out lists of airwomen and their destinations; but instead of starting with those who had to make the longest journeys and consequently the earliest starts, the whole thing was reversed. The girls called first were to travel to adjacent Lancashire towns, and had to leave the railway station the following afternoon. Once given their instructions these girls could leave the building and fill their bonus of free time as they pleased.

The officers worked through their lists, involving postings further and further away and starting times ever nearer. Finally, by four o'clock in the afternoon only a handful of us remained in the theatre. At last, my name was called with a few others; we were posted to Ashburton in Devonshire, and we were to leave on the 7.30pm train . . . that same evening.

Having idled the day away sitting in the theatre we then had to scurry back to our billets, pack and have a quick meal before dragging our kitbags to the station. Of necessity, the whole operation was completed in three hours.

CHAPTER
SEVENTEEN

Lancashire to Lincolnshire via Devonshire

I had heard that Crewe station was the largest in the world; on the journey to Ashburton I verified the fact for myself. At about midnight I hauled my kitbag for what seemed to be miles and miles; of course it could not have been more than from one end of the station to the other.

The other abiding recollection of that overnight journey was that I suffered from the head cold to end all head colds. My nose could be likened to a tap turned full on; it really was the cold of the century. We were told that a mass of inoculations over a short space of time sometimes had this effect. Paper tissues had not been invented or if they had I had not heard of them. The dozen or so linen handkerchiefs I possessed were pressed into continuous service.

At breakfast time the next morning we arrived at RAF Ashburton, the headquarters of 78 Wing. For the purposes of RDF (Radar), coverage of the country was divided into "Wings". 78 Wing covered the southwest

110

corner of the United Kingdom. We stayed at Ashburton only a day or two, using Nissen hut accommodation. The only time in my service career that I had to sleep in one of these corrugated iron structures. I was fortunate.

From Ashburton I was sent to RAF Branscombe (South Devon), a CH (Chain Home) RDF station. This was a temporary pre-training posting, designed to introduce trainees to the atmosphere of an operational station.

The need to ensure complete secrecy about our work was pressed home over and over again. No one, however near or dear, was to be given any information about the station or its operations. Local people were said to believe that the station aerials transmitted some sort of death ray. I am pretty convinced that no one ever dropped a careless word: the security was excellent.

In addition to the CH equipment, there was a connected CHL (Chain Home Low) site at nearby Beer Head. We were shown the site and the equipment, although at that stage we knew nothing of the technicalities of RDF.

Every ex-serviceman and woman will remember FFI examinations. For the uninitiated, an FFI was the check carried out by nursing staff every time one was posted, to ensure that personnel coming into the station were "Free From Infection". All parts of the body liable to horrible infections had to be inspected. Before joining up, I had not known that some of the dreaded diseases existed. Heads were included in the

111

check; one very superior girl in our group at Branscombe was found to have "nits". Although a fairly common condition in schools today, at that time it was extremely uncommon and considered a great disgrace. I remember the poor girl sobbing her heart out, so great was the shame of the discovery.

Branscombe was a pleasant station where the accommodation consisted of modern huts, each sleeping ten or twelve girls. While there, I was only eighty miles from home, and would have dearly loved to make a flying visit, but — apart from financial considerations — no amount of juggling with the bus and train timetables suggested that such a trip was possible.

When my total service amounted to six weeks, I was moved again — this time for training at RAF Cranwell.

Cranwell is, of course, a very famous Air Force establishment. Lawrence of Arabia spent time there in his Air Force era, and royal princes have undertaken training there. In wartime, it was a large establishment catering for the instruction of aircrew and various species of wireless operators.

I became part of Course 84: eighteen girls undergoing intensive training in the theory and practice of Radio Direction Finding. To use the equipment to the greatest advantage, it was essential to understand the principles of the science and how the information was converted into readable facts from the receiver screens. We worked hard, using antiquated receivers and converting all our plots manually.

We put great effort into our work, perhaps because we were told at the very beginning that the course could end in one of three ways. One could pass and be sent to an operational station; one could be labelled "FT", which meant "further training needed"; or the result could be "CT", which would indicate "you are useless and must cease training". In addition to a natural fear of an FT or CT result, two other reasons prompted me to work hard. I was mindful that I had been selected on pseudo-educational qualifications. There was also the prospect of a week's leave on completion of the training.

In addition to the technical training, we continued to spend time on drill and PT. However, all our serious concentration was centred on the radar work, and the drill sessions became mindless frolics. Already our mentors seemed to have accepted that the less formal aspects of service training took second place; our technical role was to be the vital one.

Drill was just fun, especially when we got it all wrong. A few people turning right instead of left on the parade ground can cause no end of merriment and confusion. Equally, a squad which pretends not to hear the drill corporal's instruction, and goes on marching, marching into the brick wall at the end of the parade ground, reduces the participants to a state of helpless mirth.

Now we no longer considered ourselves to be "rookies".

There were plenty of the opposite sex at Cranwell and social opportunities abounded. The facilities of the huge station were excellent; there were NAAFIs, dance halls, cinemas and entertainments of all kinds. We were allowed a certain number of passes to leave the camp when not working, and generally we began to enjoy a welcome degree of freedom.

As required by the fashion of the day, I wore my hair softly permed and longish. While at Cranwell my hair needed attention to achieve that essential requirement of the women's services, "hair must be off the collar". I decided to have one of the station hairdresser's perms. It was inexpensive and a disaster. Despite my firm instruction that the perm must be very loose, the result was a ghastly wire-wool effect.

One of the girls wrote a poem about our course, devoting a few lines to each member. I think the matter of trying to cope with my wire-wool hair may have accounted in part for the impression the poem gives that I spent my time before the mirror! But then again I have always tended to be vain — and she was certainly right about "and thinks of the men".

Anyway here is the poem:

The Tale Of Course 84

This is the story of Course 84,
The course that shook Cranwell as never before.
So listen a minute, a tale I will tell
Of seventeen wee Waafies who got on so well.

Now there's Arnold, that girl we call Gwen,
Who looks in the mirror and thinks of the men.

Ball was the girl who was always late
And caught up the squad outside the gate.

Dancing was more in the line of Jean Bell,
Especially with Czechs, whom she liked very well.
Now Scotland produced a wee bonnie lass
Named Carey, and gee how she stepped on the gas.

If ever a girl deserved writer's cramp,
'Twas Daniels who wrote by the light of the lamp.
There was Davis, who one day was late for lunch,
Excused PT but still the last of the bunch.

Hicks was the girl who to Lincoln did go,
She said to be confirmed, but you never know.
Fisher and Mitchell the heavenly twin,
Always together, outdoors and in.

Now Kyle was the girl who believed in a jest,
That bed at all times, was definitely best.
With Kathy from Glasgow you could always depend,
Would decide to join you right at the end.

With Langton we agreed it was all very sad,
As we watched her cough as it grew very bad.
Dorothy Rawle on this poem much time has spent
And hopes you will take it the way it is meant.

A canny lass from Newcastle did hail,
Margaret Scott who was always sure she would fail.
The company of Shute we haven't tonight,
With Ian she went twigging by the pale moonlight.

Alas and alack the measles did strike,
And with Wallinton went a girl we did like.
"It's six o'clock chaps" comes from the end of the room,
'Twas White who was always first with the broom.

To our corporals a tribute we really must pay.
They gave us the "gen" by night and by day.
Now all that is left is our midnight feast,
Then home we shall go for seven days at least.

Much fun we have had, you will all agree.
So think of the hut by the old gooseberry tree.
And so as we say "Good Bye and Good Luck",
We hope we shall meet when our six months is up.

Dorothy Rawle.

I have a photograph of Course 84 and remember most of the girls very well.

There was Jean Bell, a dark-haired London girl who was very good looking and wore dramatic make-up, but I remember most her ability to dress completely while still under the bedclothes. It was March-April time and cold; but Jean did not bare herself to the atmosphere, she simply wriggled under the blankets for a few minutes, and then stepped out fully clothed. How she coped with her ablutions, I really do not know.

A gentle girl named Jean Kyle cried softly when news of her fiancé's death was received, but then carried on, making no fuss at all.

The writer of the poem, Dorothy Rawle, later became one of my dearest friends. I did not know Dorothy very well at Cranwell, but we were to move to our next posting together and our friendship has endured.

One course member, Evelyn White, seemed much older than the rest of us. She was, I suspect, about 28, but when you are hardly out of your teens twenty-eight or nine seems ancient and "past it". Evelyn got things done, and my strongest recollection is of her leaping out of bed at the first note of the Tannoy, and yelling "First with the broom!" Her bed space was then swept before she performed any other part of the morning routine. Only one broom was provided, and each girl had to sweep the linoleum surrounding her bed before leaving for the cookhouse. Evelyn made sure that no broom queue would ever make her late for breakfast.

The proportion of men to girls at Cranwell was favourable. At the station dances, the plainest girl could be sure of dancing from the first note of the band's performance to the last.

At one such dance I met Donald, a newly appointed Pilot Officer training to be an aircrew wireless operator. He was a tall, plumpish lad with a round face; not an academic person, he had already been FT'd on his course. I had the impression that his training was being drawn out over months and months. Nevertheless he was an exceedingly likeable boy. I understood that his parents owned a cotton mill in Lancashire; he clearly came from a "good" family.

Donald was gentle and sensitive. He loved the music of Chopin and played the piano with great feeling. It was he who introduced me to Chopin, and to this day I take delight in the sensuous beauty of the Berceuse and the Ballades of this most romantic of composers.

Some evenings Donald and I "broke into" the vast gymnasium at Cranwell, and there Donald would play the piano for two or three hours for our mutual pleasure.

Several times during my six-week stay at Cranwell, Donald and I spent the day in Lincoln. The trip usually ended with dinner at either "The White Hart" or "The Saracen's Head". Dining out was an activity I had indulged in very little up to that time. Despite the restrictions of wartime Britain, the fare provided by these two hostelries was outstandingly good. Refinements like taking liqueurs with coffee at the end of a meal were all so new to me, but I learnt rapidly and enjoyed every minute of it.

The "White Hart" or "Saracen's Head" was chosen because each boasted a grand piano in its dining-room. We arranged to dine latish in the appointed dining period, and sat on until the dining-room emptied. Donald would then ask to be allowed to use the piano. Permission was always given. For an hour or so I listened to Chopin played with Donald's lovely gentle touch. Even 1940s Hollywood could not equal the romantic atmosphere.

I was not in love with Donald but perhaps a little spellbound by the new world he showed me. We corresponded after I left Cranwell, and later in the war years he was to have a part to play in my life.

The last week of the training found the members of Course 84 very worried indeed. We were examined in both the theory and the practice of the science of Radar, in order to decide whether we had passed, were designated "FT" — or horror of horrors — "CT". Happily, tied with Margaret Mitchell I came top of the course.

The first three months of service life completed, Course 84 broke up for a week of well-deserved leave. For my part, I had longed to be back with my family and the time at home passed all too quickly. Mother was comforted to have me back looking well and plump, and when at the end of the week I donned my uniform again it no longer felt strange.

CHAPTER
EIGHTEEN

Bawdsey

My posting was to RAF Bawdsey in Suffolk . . . and how fortunate I was! Bawdsey Manor is idyllically situated on the northern side of the estuary of the River Deben. Bawdsey village is two or three miles inland to the north, while the little town of Felixstowe is across the river and three miles south. The estate can be reached by road from Woodbridge, but by far the more convenient approach is by road from Felixstowe and across the Deben by boat.

The manor house was built by Sir Cuthbert Quilter in 1890, and purchased by the Air Ministry in 1935 for £24,000. It was there that Sir Watson Watt carried out experimental work and developed RDF, later to be known as Radar. It was exciting to be posted to the original Radar station; the place where an invention that changed the course of the war was born.

The house is built in a mixture of styles and is of no great architectural interest. It is set in 168 acres of wooded land, which also contains many small houses, stables and even a derelict church; well-tended little formal gardens are dotted about the grounds. In 1943, summerhouses, relics of the days when the manor was a private residence, abounded, and the cliff walks were generously supplied with man-made seats and alcoves.

The Red and White towers are a feature of the house, each tower being topped by a group of four turrets. The White Tower, built on oriental lines, contained small, rather barren rooms that we believed to have previously been servants' quarters. However, when at Bawdsey recently, I was told that the White Tower had been designed to accommodate the children of the family.

The pseudo-Elizabethan Red Tower is very grand, and has magnificent views of river and sea. No doubt, the Quilter family used this part of the house, as most of the bedrooms in the Red Tower are fitted with ornate cupboards and wardrobes, luxuries undreamed of by the wartime inmates. The bathrooms in the Red Tower are most impressive; one, known as "the Baron's bathroom", boasted gold-plated taps and elaborate fittings of nautical design.

The Gothic-styled section of the building between the towers consisted of large panelled rooms, which, in 1943, were for the most part used as offices and orderly rooms. Two of the larger rooms functioned as sleeping accommodation for the non-technical WAAF personnel. One room that retained its original purpose by becoming the venue for many social activities was the panelled ballroom. The most important event was the regular Sunday evening dance.

In my time, although sparsely furnished with RAF furniture, the manor was a hundred times more comfortable than conventional service accommodation. Central heating was installed and the palatial original bathrooms augmented by many adequate, if more austere ones. A small part of the manor was used as officers' quarters, but mainly it was the home of the WAAF personnel.

The men of the RAF were accommodated in various buildings in the grounds. Some shared cottages situated near the ferry —- these were known as "married quarters". Others lived in various estate cottages, one of which was labelled "laundry cottage" and another "honeymoon cottage". There were also a few typical service huts hidden away in the woods.

Today it is probably difficult to understand the then prevailing concept of keeping young men and young women completely segregated. For my part, I never went anywhere near the men's quarters. It would have been most improper to be seen heading in the general direction of the men's billets. And male forays into the manor were limited to attending the Sunday evening dances in the ballroom and while there, if invited, taking a cup of coffee in the WAAF "Naafi".

When fellow Course 84 member Dorothy Rawle and I arrived at Felixstowe station towards the end of April 1943, we immediately made the acquaintance of the ferry bus service. The "fleet" consisted of two vehicles, which even by 1943 standards looked frail and antique. They were privately owned, and driven by the owner, a Mr Aldous, and an employee named Albert. Throughout the journeys Albert talked incessantly in strong Suffolk brogue, addressing the passengers in general, but seldom, if ever, did they comprehend a word of what he said.

The ancient buses, hand-painted in sky blue, shuttled between Felixstowe town and the Deben estuary. The service was good and carefully synchronised to meet the RAF ferryboat that crossed the river every half hour from early morning until 11.30pm. Both bus and boat were lifelines for the Bawdsey folk, and greatly appreciated.

So Dorothy and I found our way to Bawdsey Manor by making the first of countless trips across the Deben. Getting our strong service shoes wet, we boarded the RAF motorboat for the first time. Later we were to learn that by scrambling over the side of the boat in a certain way and quickly, the wetting could be limited to one foot! We came to enjoy our almost daily boat trips; whether the water was being whipped up by strong winds, causing us to pull hats down over ears and tuck chins well down into greatcoat collars, or whether the sun shone and sparkled on the gentle river. Perhaps our enjoyment was greatest when romantically, on moonlit nights, the boat left a phosphorescent wash behind it.

For the first time we leapt from the side of the ferryboat onto the wet sandy shore, and booked in at the little guardroom by the water's edge.

We struggled the three or four hundred yards along the tree-lined path to the manor, dragging our kitbags behind us. We were immediately impressed by the grandeur of our surroundings, and when the manor house itself came into view, I think we realised that we were very fortunate to be posted there.

We were installed in room 54, one of the less grand rooms at the top of the White Tower. The room contained five double bunk beds and one single bed. We were allocated a bunk bed in one of the turrets. I won the toss for the top bunk and so was able to enjoy views from windows on three sides.

Cpl Anne Downing, a great character who hailed from Cornwall, occupied the only single bed. Anne, the daughter of a clergyman, was a complex girl, plump, very jolly and the possessor of a vocabulary of swear words, many of which were quite unknown to me at the time. By the standards of my narrow-minded upbringing, no young lady swore! However, there was another side to Anne's character; every night she knelt by her bed and said her prayers. In my three and a half years of service life, I saw no other colleague do this. Anne was a bright, entertaining girl and loved by everyone.

A tall attractive girl named Betty occupied the top bunk of the bed by the door. Her husband had been overseas for a long time; after years of loyalty, she had become friendly with a soldier from a neighbouring gun site. Unworldly as I undoubtedly was, I remember registering shock when Betty came in one night slightly the worse for drink, clothing very "disarranged" and only able to climb onto her top bunk with a lot of help from the rest of us. How great the strain must have been for young married people separated for years by the war.

124

* * *

There were three types of radar equipment at Bawdsey: CH (Chain Home), CHL (Chain Home Low) and "K" (designed to pick up low-flying aircraft and shipping).

Dorothy and I became members of "C" watch at the CH site. The four-watch system started with an 11pm to 8am night watch, and was followed by a 6pm to 11pm evening watch on the same day. The next day we worked from 1pm to 6pm, and the following day from 8am to 1pm. We were then free until the night watch on the following evening, which gave a break of 34 hours.

The accepted procedure was to take a meal en route to the operations block, and another on the way back to the manor at the end of the watch. The "cookhouse", a converted stable, was conveniently placed between the manor and the operations block. The food was not good. Large RAF stations boasted well-qualified cooks, but ours, being a small unit of about a hundred bodies, had a lowly corporal in charge. At times, the food provided was barely edible.

The occupants of room 54 were employed at various sites and watches, making sleeping after night watch difficult, but the young adjust to circumstances easily and we did not suffer from sleeplessness to any serious degree.

Sometimes when coming off night watch via the cookhouse, we "stole" bread, butter and marmalade for our roommates, who, if they had been on watch until 11pm the previous evening, rarely got up for breakfast. The radar mechanics kept us supplied with adequate electric heaters (elements in jam tins), which enabled us to make toast and boil water; many an enjoyable breakfast of tea, toast and marmalade was provided in this way.

Such homemade heaters were of course forbidden, being an obvious fire risk. Even so, the appetising smell of freshly made toast often pervaded the manor; it was remarkable that the officers seemed to lack a sense of smell and we always got away with this misdeed.

One day we had a very near miss. The WAAF CO sprang an inspection on us when a homemade heater, still hot from use, was standing on the floor. Dorothy, with great presence of mind, dropped a cardigan over the heater. We were criticised for being untidy, but got away with the greater crime of possessing a heater. For three awful minutes, I expected the cardigan to go up in flames. The CO didn't even appear to notice the pungent smell of burning wool!

When off duty for 34 hours between watches, we often took sleeping-out passes. Sometimes we simply booked ourselves into a hostel in Felixstowe, and there enjoyed a few hours of near luxury, civilian style. On other occasions, we hitch-hiked to Ipswich or Norwich, where we would sightsee or perhaps visit the theatre, again staying overnight in a hostel run by the YMCA or a Church charity. Hitch-hiking was considered an acceptable method of travel for girls in those days. Usually we travelled in twos, but there were times when I hitch-hiked alone. Did we take terrible risks, or were people just so much more worthy of trust in those days?

As far as work was concerned, I made quite an auspicious start. After completing five months at Bawdsey, we were required to take further technical examinations. I managed to do well; a boy named Alan Seal and I both achieved over 80% and jumped a rank by going in one step from ACW2 to LACW. All the other contenders either made the intermediate rank of ACW1 or had to take the examination again.

CHAPTER
NINETEEN

Operational

The work at Bawdsey was both exciting and interesting, there being plenty of enemy activity over East Anglia. Our sets could "see" nearly 200 miles across the North Sea. Enemy aircraft were picked up as the planes left Holland and plotted right across the sea until they reached the English coast. Our fighters were quickly on the scene, having been guided finally by another type of Radar — GCI (Ground Control Interception) — and brought into close contact with their targets. Meanwhile, we continued to plot everything in the area, but watching particularly the track of the hostile plane as it intermingled with that of our fighter, until the moment came when the echoes were actually beating together.

Seconds later, where there had been two tracks only one remained. Anxiously we watched for an extra blip — IFF (Identification Friend or Foe) — which was transmitted only by friendly aircraft, always hoping so much that it was not "our" plane which had been shot down.

The IFF signal was also important when planes were in distress; the signal could be adjusted by the pilot to give a broad blip, which was the official SOS signal.

We all watched very carefully for broad IFF, and when it was reported the Filter Officer at Stanmore often requested us to concentrate on the aircraft in distress. Other nearby and overlapping stations would be left to deal with the general activity, while we threw up plot after plot on the plane that was in trouble. Often such planes lost height rapidly and limped in very slowly. If, alas, the echo disappeared from our screens, it usually meant that the plane was "in the drink". The accuracy of our last plot was vital to enable the rescue services to pinpoint the search area.

On happier occasions the "broad IFF" plane crossed the coast sometimes only marginally higher than the treetops and our aerials. If we could spare a "body" from the watch, he or she would be sent outside to see, and hear the crippled plane flying over us.

Quite recently I discovered that there was a "crash" aerodrome at Woodbridge which was specially equipped to deal with planes landing in a damaged state. It speaks well for wartime security that, although we were situated so close by, we knew nothing of the existence of this crash 'drome. With hindsight it is obvious that the "SOS" planes which we so often plotted were making for Woodbridge.

In time, our own aircraft came to predominate, until literally hundreds of British and American bombers swept across the North Sea every day. At night the bomber force was often preceded by a dozen or so Mosquitoes, flying at great speed and height in single file, twenty or thirty miles apart. The Pathfinder Mosquitoes were the only aircraft type we could

129

identify; the wooden construction of the planes gave an unusual beating response. One of the WAAF supervisors was married to a Mosquito pilot; when she was on duty we all quietly counted the Mosquitoes out, and counted them back in again, Falklands style.

The greatest number of aircraft I saw on the screen at one time was 1,950+; my estimation of the number was not disputed by Stanmore, in fact we were congratulated on the accuracy of our estimation. (I have since looked at the official records in the Public Records Office at Kew, and find that on 10.2.45 when 1900+ planes took part in raids, Stanmore congratulated Bawdsey on its estimation. This could well have been the same day.) On that occasion, the planes were mainly friendly, but intermingled were a handful of single tracks labelled "X" (Unknown), and a few identified as "H" (Hostile).

It is strange how little we fretted about the reality of war and its horror. It did not worry me that each bomber carried a full load of bombs that would spell death and disaster somewhere. We had seen the ruins of British cities bombed by the enemy, and we knew all about the British lives lost in the terrible raids of the early months of the war. To us the raids made by the Allies were just a necessary part of bringing the whole ghastly business to an end. We prayed for the safety of those nearest and dearest to us and for our country, but that was all. War was a necessary evil — to be lived through and won.

Looking back, it is surprising how accustomed to it

all we became. Similarly, today we constantly hear of murder in Ireland, South Africa and the Middle East, and hardly register the reality of it all. Trauma that goes on and on becomes accepted as almost inevitable. We were part of the fighting forces and we were glad to be helping to win the battle. On a personal level, it meant getting on with the war, getting it over and returning home. Although without doubt we had tremendous fun, and for many it proved to be the most interesting part of their lives, everyone I knew longed for the day when it would all be over, and we could return to our normal ways of life.

Bawdsey was, of course, a legitimate target and we were bombed and strafed a few times. Strangely, I felt little fear. At home, in the early months of the war when the enemy bombers had droned over Bournemouth all night, I sat in the cupboard under the stairs with my mother and sister, physically shaking with fear. At Bawdsey, I was unmoved. Perhaps at home my fears were for my dear ones and our home and not so much for myself.

CHAPTER
TWENTY

24 Hours At Bawdsey Radar Station November 1944

by LACW Joan Lancaster

This is an account written by a great friend of mine, Joan Lancaster, now Mrs Dingwall. Joan wrote this for her grandson when he was a member of the ATC, and when I met up with Joan recently, after losing touch for more than forty years, she showed this account to me. It is so accurate and so vividly brought back the atmosphere of those days that I asked her if I could include it in my story of Bawdsey; Joan agreed and here it is.

MIDNIGHT. I have been on duty for one hour and my eyes are telling me I should be in bed, but there is a long night ahead until we go off duty at 08.00hrs. Three large RAF raids have been to Germany earlier in the evening, many aircraft have returned, but there are now a number of stragglers on our radar screen. Many will be in difficulty and judging by their heights some are already dangerously low, and liable to ditch into the sea. We continuously plot and track each one in turn, praying that they make it to the coastline.

01.20hrs. A faint blip appears at 115 miles, the start of a new track. Find the bearing, press buttons and the grid reference plot number comes up on the display panel. It's just off the Dutch coast. Switch over to the height aerials, find the height, press more buttons — height 20,000 feet. Study the blip and estimate 40+ aircraft. Pass the information through to the Plotter in Filter room and thence to Group Headquarters. Very soon we receive back the identification HOSTILE Track No 153. Take more plots — range now 100 miles, height still 20,000ft, but now estimate 60+ aircraft. Pass information through and keep track on our own plotting table.

Most of our RAF planes have now come in, but one disappeared from the radar screen at 20 miles from the coast. The plane must have gone down. We visualise the aircrew scrambling out from their sinking plane. What if one of them is unconscious? Have they all managed to get into the dinghy? Will Air Sea Rescue find them?

HOSTILE 153 — Plot, range 80 miles, height 18,000ft. Now estimate 75+ aircraft. Keep tracking. Keep tracking. Detect new blip at 3 miles going out. Looks like two aircraft. Take plots. Identified Friendly — RAF. We track them going out 8 miles, 10 miles, 15 miles. They stop at 20 miles and turn, then stooge around between 18 and 22 miles. Back and forth, round and round. Must be the Air Sea Rescue bods looking for that crew that ditched. Keep watching.

HOSTILE 153 — Plot, range 50 miles, height 15,000 ft. 75+ aircraft. Keep close watch — 40 miles, 30 miles, 20 miles. By the look of the track on the plotting table they appear to be heading straight for us! The Plotter on the other end of the line jokes: "Hope you've got your tin hats on, it's been nice knowing you!" Quickly take more plots — the blip is beginning to fade fast at 15 miles, two further plots indicate they have veered south-east and should shortly cross our coastline. Looks as if they could be heading for London. The ack-ack will be ready for them and the air-raid warning system alerted. We give a sigh of relief, we're safe this time, anyway.

02.00hrs. Suddenly there is a call from the WAAF sitting at the other Radar set — Code named OSWALD. A rocket has just taken off from its base. It is showing very clearly, and rising in a straight line — information quickly passed to Group — the rocket climbs steadily, high into the stratosphere, then gradually curves over at the top of its flight path and very slowly begins to fade from the screen. It is now overhead and going overland behind us on its way to its destination. In a further two minutes it will have dropped to earth — nobody knows where it will fall, we can only watch helplessly, the RAF has no defence against these V2 rockets.

At last all of our own stragglers have crossed the coastline, but we still have the two aircraft stooging round at 20 miles.

02.35hrs. Another rocket, followed by a further one at 02.50.

03.00hrs. We now have a blank screen, the two RAF who were at 20 miles have now returned to base. We hope they found the ditched crew. It is also time for us to move into different positions in the Ops. room. One hour is long enough to keep one's eyes glued to the Radar screen. The WAAF who was plotting now goes "On the Tube" (watches the radar screen) and the rest of us take various positions as Plotter at the grid reference map, Teller /Recorder who passes every single plot and all the information through to the Filter room, and records the exact time and plots. Another WAAF takes over watching the Oswald screen for the rockets.

We each have one hour's break during the night when we make tea for the rest of the watch if wanted, or we can sit at a table and rest our heads on our arms and snatch a little sleep, although this is not usually a good idea as when woken an hour later one feels absolutely dreadful. It really is better to try to keep awake and alert.

03.10hrs. "DIVER, DIVER!" the WAAF at the Radar screen calls out loudly. It's the code name for the V1 Flying Bomb which has just appeared. It looks exactly the same as an aircraft blip, but after a few seconds' observation it will be seen to be flying much too fast for a plane. It races along the Radar screen at 500 miles per hour (aircraft flew at approx 300mph). Take

135

several plots in succession — yes, it's keeping a dead straight course, no pilot to take evasive action. Range 40 miles, 30 miles, 20 miles. Another one detected at 40 miles, same speed, same height, same course 30 miles, 20 miles. First one now coming in fast to Zero — should be overhead, keep our fingers crossed its engine doesn't cut out — we don't want it diving on us! More picked up at 50 miles, 46 miles, and at 41 miles.

A new track now going out is identified as RAF: 6+ going out to deal with those flying bombs. They turn around before reaching them and fly alongside for a few seconds to turn them away. Some disappear from the radar screen — GOOD SHOW! Others are still rushing in.

04.05hrs. Last of the flying bombs gone overland, and the RAF returned.

04.12hrs. Another rocket detected. The range is further away than the previous ones, so it must have been launched from a different site. We look at the clock. In four minutes' time it will crash to earth and will devastate a large area of London, and maybe kill hundreds. We try not to think about it.

04.23hrs. We pick up a track on the edge of our radar coverage. RAF, 100+ returning from a raid, look to be making for an airfield in Kent. We keep track for twenty minutes and then it fades. It will have been plotted by another radar station further south.

04.50hrs. ROCKET

05.12hrs. ROCKET

05.30hrs. The screen is coming to life again, large blips emerging from Zero range, and all moving from us towards Belgium and Holland. We know what they are — it's the USAAF taking off in their huge Flying Fortresses, the B17s, from their bases in the countryside around us in Suffolk and the rest of East Anglia.

The screen is now a solid mass from Zero to 30 miles, extending outwards every minute. The blips all moving in one direction — towards Germany. We try to make out individual tracks, but it's impossible. Soon those German towns and military installations will be getting a good pounding. Every morning the Fortresses set out for their daylight mass bombing of Germany. We hope to God they drop a few bombs on those Flying Bomb and Rocket sites as they pass overhead!

06.00hrs. The radar screen is a solid mass, the leading edge of the Fortresses beginning to fade from our screen as they go beyond our radar coverage. The screen will be solid for another hour or so yet.

Outside, the rest of the camp will be awake. It is impossible to sleep through the continuous thunder of low-flying heavy aircraft, but the sight is magnificent; planes as far as the eye can see, hundreds of them, some low, some higher up, all crossing the coastline and making out across sea. They will be back later in the day when the next watch will plot them coming home again.

08.00hrs. At last our night watch is over. The next crew arrives and takes over from us. We feel very weary — too tired to eat much breakfast; sometimes we cannot face it at all. All we want is to get to bed. We sleep solidly until about 2 or 3pm, then up for a bath, time to write a letter perhaps before having tea at 5pm. Then back on duty for the evening watch 6pm-11pm.

18.00hrs. We take over from the afternoon crew. They have had considerable activity all afternoon and there are many large blips on the radar screen at the moment. We take up our positions one by one and continue the plotting and tracking without a break.

18.30 hrs. We begin to get a much larger build-up of aircraft leaving our shores. It's the RAF this time going out on their night raids to Germany. They keep nice tight formations, and we can track them properly, not like the Yanks who spread themselves out all over the place, or so it appears on the radar screen. 100+ going South East. 250+ due East. 50+ SSE and half an hour later 400+ due East again. We continue to plot and track every formation until they fade away off our screen at 80 — 100 — 120 miles. They will be crossing the enemy coastline by now with ack-ack shells exploding all around their aircraft. Please God, keep them safe.

20.10hrs. A rocket, followed by three more before 21.30. Hitler hasn't given up yet. Hope the RAF are giving him hell.

21.40hrs. Faint blips appear at range 80 miles. We take plots and range and height and await identification. Hostile or Friendly? They're friendly — must be the first of the RAF on their way back.

22.05hrs. We begin to get very busy as more and more returning aircraft show up. The formations are not so neat as when they left, they've no doubt had a rough time. 20+ here, 30+ there. No matter, as long as they all get back. The WAAF Radar Operator works her way along the length of the radar trace plotting every blip, then back to the beginning again. Plot, range, height 50+ — plot, range, height 25+ — plot, range, height 100+. One lone aircraft at 40 miles, very low, coming in very slowly. Must keep a constant track of this one — 30 miles — 25 miles.

23.00hrs. The night watch has arrived. They take over our positions after we have familiarised them with the tracks being plotted at the moment, especially our lone straggler.

23.00hrs. We collect our belongings then out into the night, take a few gulps of real fresh air and then make for the cookhouse. It's deserted, but an urn of cocoa, some thick white bread and some golden syrup has been left out for us. We are more tired than hungry, but have a bite to eat and some cocoa — Ugh! It's too strong, too sweet and needs more milk. We make our way back to the living quarters — all quiet now — everyone else asleep.

23.30 hrs. Get into pyjamas, clean teeth, wash, comb hair and creep into bed.

23.45 hrs. Mentally plan tomorrow. Off duty in the morning so MUST get clean sheets, give bedspace a good clean and tidy bedside cupboard — can't find a thing. Oh! nearly forgot, a pile of washing waiting to be done. Also press battledress trousers. Should just have time for a bath before early lunch at midday. On duty 1pm to 6pm. Have tea and back here by 7pm. Too late to go off camp. Someone said there's a film show at 8 o'clock. Might go. Hope it's not one of those films about the RAF bombing Germany! Must get to sleep . . .

CHAPTER
TWENTY-ONE

Misdeeds

Dorothy and I remained on the same watch and continued to spend most of our free time together. Social activities involved crossing the ferry to visit Felixstowe or to travel further afield. Occasionally, with the rest of the watch, we spent an evening at one of the two pubs on the other side of the river. Prior to joining up I had never entered a public house in my life, but I quickly discovered what I had been missing. Recently after an absence of over forty years, I discovered that the Ferry Boat Inn is still in existence and has hardly changed. In 1943 the "Vic" and the "Ferry Boat" were well patronised by Bawdsey folk; mostly good-tempered, happy young people making a few drinks last all the evening. Of course, there would occasionally be one or two who got a bit carried away, and certainly it was not unknown for a reveller to slip when climbing into the ferryboat. Often, the late night crossings of the Deben were both funny and entertaining.

In very rough weather the RAF boat could not negotiate the currents of the river, and on such occasions personnel had to stay in camp or find entertainment in Bawdsey village or Woodbridge. There was no public transport to either of these places, so it was a matter of cycling or hitch-hiking. One Sunday morning Dorothy and I set out to go to church in Felixstowe, but the estuary was too rough for the boat to cross, so we borrowed bicycles and pedalled to the tiny church in Bawdsey village. Counting the vicar there were six people in church. The singing was thin and reedy and when the time came for the sermon, the vicar solemnly announced that as there were so few people present, he was going to save his sermon for next week. I regret to say that Dorothy and I disgraced ourselves by giggling audibly.

One day after Dorothy and I had spent our off-duty time in Ipswich, we attempted to hitch-hike back to Felixstowe, but alas there was little traffic on the road and we had minimal success. Eventually, we had to use some of that very scarce commodity — money — to make the journey by train. We managed to get as far as Orwell village in a truck which smelled strongly of fish, but from there we had no option but to sit in the little station and wait for the last train. We arrived in Felixstowe too late to catch Albert's last bus, and had to spend yet more money on a taxi. As if to prove that nothing was to go right for us that day, we reached the water's edge to see the last ferry of the day (the 11.30pm), halfway across the river.

Although we had late passes we were required to be in camp by midnight. Somehow we had to get across the water. We banged on the door of a fisherman's tiny cottage and pleaded with him to row us across.

As he dressed, a tirade of grumbles in a strong Suffolk brogue penetrated the thin wooden walls of the cottage. Eventually, he emerged and still grumbling rowed us to the other side of the river. The journey made this way took far longer than by the motorised RAF boat, and when we arrived on the Manor side it was already ten minutes past midnight. The fee asked by the fisherman was two shillings; this paid, he kissed Dorothy firmly on the cheek by way of a bonus.

For booking in ten minutes late Dorothy and I were put on our first charge. The next morning with due ceremony we were marched before the WAAF CO. After telling the story of our efforts to get back to camp on time, we were given the lightest possible punishment — a reprimand. Our escort, one Nancy Partington, giggled throughout the ridiculous proceedings, for which she received a far greater telling-off than we did.

Later, after Dorothy had been posted away from Bawdsey, I committed another "grave offence" and was charged again. My "crime" this time occurred one perfect summer's evening when walking with a boyfriend, from Bawdsey village to the camp. I had rashly removed my hat and my boyfriend was carrying it in the hand furthest from me, when the WAAF CO rounded the bend in the road and walked towards us. It would have looked ridiculous to grab the hat and ram it on my head, so I carried on walking and smiled my acknowledgment. The offence of walking out minus hat was compounded by the fact that I was unable to salute (without a hat an airwoman was improperly dressed, and to salute one must be properly dressed). The sentence this time was two days confined to camp, which was no great hardship because I had watches to perform on both days and so would not have left camp in any case.

These two minor offences meant that when I left the service my character was recorded as "very good", while my husband who was more adept at not being found out, had "excellent" on his record. I was not allowed to forget!

In the 1940s, unlike today, the sexes were very strictly segregated. Male personnel were allowed to enter the Manor only on Sunday evenings when the weekly dance took place. They were then confined to the ballroom and the WAAF NAAFI. The "Waaf Naaf" was a small NAAFI which occupied a room on the ground floor of the Manor, and which was strictly out of bounds to the RAF the other six days of the week. As a great concession and if accompanied by a WAAF, men were allowed to move between the ballroom and the NAAFI, and there permitted to refresh themselves with coffee and buns.

There was however one isolated occasion when a member of the RAF did penetrate the WAAF quarters. Had he been caught, I cannot contemplate the punishment that would have followed.

It happened like this. Late one night I was sitting up in my top bunk bed, gloriously attired in my frumpish "issue" pyjamas, when the door of room 54 burst open. In tumbled Cpl Anne Downing, in very exuberant mood having spent the evening in the Ferry

Boat Inn. Behind her came one AC Jimmy Kimber. Normally, Jimmy was a shy retiring lad, but on this occasion he too had reinforced his courage with quantities of the local ale.

The inmates of room 54 were dumbfounded. No male had ever been seen in WAAF sleeping quarters before. Jimmy rushed up to my bed, kissed me firmly on the lips and rushed out again like a frightened rabbit. LACW Peggy Butler, who had been posted in that day, breathed, "So this is what goes on at Bawdsey!"

Both Anne and Jimmy took risks they would not normally have dreamed of taking. Fortunately, they were not seen entering the Manor by a side door and stumbling up two long flights of stairs.

Today the story is not worth relating; in 1943 the sleeping quarters of the other sex were totally out of bounds. Room 54 was certainly amazed. If a kangaroo had hopped into the room, they could not have been more surprised!

From time to time we indulged in an exercise known as a "Stand To". This was a 48-hour practice in how to deal with invasion by the enemy. I suppose it was necessary because we were vulnerable, being a highly secret installation perched on a coastline which had little cliff or natural defence of any kind.

Everyone was confined to camp for as long as the "Stand To" lasted, and as far as we were concerned it was all a great bore. The wretched exercise meant that if not on watch, personnel were designated to various duties, such as stretcher-bearer, first aider or guard. The meals, always poor at Bawdsey, were reduced to uncooked or half cooked "iron rations". It was all very tedious and unnecessary in the opinion of most of us.

I was fairly useless as a stretcher-bearer, but that was unimportant because most of the time the duty involved just sitting in the room marked "Stretcher Bearers". But once we did have a casualty, when a very large airman developed influenza while on watch. The chap was quite capable of walking to Sick Bay or to his billet, but to add realism to the "Stand To", the stretcher-bearers were sent to carry him to Sick Bay. It was a long walk and I regret to say that my arms were not up to the task. My corner of the stretcher got lower and lower, until eventually I dropped it altogether and the poor unfortunate airman rolled onto the mud. He then sensibly elected to walk to Sick Bay, while the four useless stretcher-bearers shuffled behind with the empty stretcher.

During another 48-hour "Stand To", the practice air raid warning had sounded and Dorothy and I, being off duty, had to take our places in the official shelter. Our appointed bolthole was a 30-yard, man-made tunnel, which ran from the main road leading to the Manor, through to a back path which led to a little-used rear door of the Manor. After standing around in this very dull tunnel for an hour or so, we realised that the time appointed for the opening of the "Waaf Naaf" had arrived.

Why not slip out of the back end of the tunnel into the little-used rear entrance to the Manor, thence to the "Naaf" and there to enjoy an illicit cup of coffee. No one noticed our departure and ten minutes later, refreshed, we slipped back into the tunnel just in time to see the last three of the sheltering WAAFs all geared up in anti-gas clothing, "tin" hats and gas masks, running out of the front end of the tunnel. We had not heard the gas alert!

Hastily we unpacked our gas capes, put them on, donned our gas masks and "tin" hats, rushed through the tunnel and down the drive trying to catch up the main party who were making for a gas dugout in the woods. Ever tried running and giggling in a service gas mask? The more you laugh and pant, the more the rubber sides of the mask flap and honk, making indescribable noises. The greater the noise the more we laughed. Oh to be young and to find everything so funny! My mother used to say "when you're young you laugh to see a pudding crawl", although I must say I've never understood the statement.

In April 1944, Dorothy was posted to Beer Head in Devon. I missed her very much, but as an established Bawdseyite was given an opportunity to move to the Red Tower. This was a big improvement. I then had a single bed under the window of a large room that was beautifully equipped with fitted cupboards and wardrobes — all very civilised and pleasant. Just four of us shared the room, which had superb views of the Deben estuary and the North Sea. It is from this period of my life that I derived my longing to live within the sight and sound of the sea.

We hired a wireless set, brought pillows from home and now having access to "the Baron's bathroom", began to live a life of comparative luxury.

My companions in room 18 were Joan Lancaster, Alice Murley and Peggy Butler. Alice was a pharmacist in civilian life and much older than the rest of us. I expect that she was then about 39 or 40. At the time I thought her very ancient. Now, when we exchange news at Christmas time, she is a contemporary. Joan and I became great friends, but unfortunately, we lost touch with each other over the years. (In 1993 I made contact with Joan again, hence Joan's *Twenty-Four Hours at Bawdsey Radar Station.*) Peggy was very much into the literary world and still is, I understand. She was madly in love with an American at the time; now, two husbands later, she lives in Sussex. I hear from her every Christmas and recently met her again. She has changed very little in the intervening forty years.

CHAPTER
TWENTY-TWO

Romances

I met scores of young men whilst at Bawdsey. They often wanted serious affairs, but I belonged to a generation which believed that true love came only once in a lifetime. I had been programmed not to indulge in numerous romances and felt that casual flirtations would detract from the real thing — when it came. I was quite sure that the real thing would happen one day. A great many of my generation felt as I did. We had lots of "fun", certainly enjoyed male company, but unlike today's young women we were sparing with our favours. Some of the boys I dated proposed marriage (shades of Barbara Cartland), but I always said "no" and went on waiting for the "great romance". Hollywood led us to believe that that was the normal way of things. Once in every lifetime the "great romance" just happened. In some mystic way I would be sure to know when my moment came. I did not exactly expect a string orchestra to tune up, but I did think that a wonderful aura would engulf me and that everything would be blissful. If only I had been more realistic!

In the meantime, in common with my companions I worked hard; equally, I played hard. The social event of the week was the Sunday evening dance in the Manor ballroom. I always managed to spend some time at this function, albeit only an hour when on the 6pm to 11pm watch. Always an enthusiastic dancer, watch permitting, I would be one of the first to arrive, hoping to have one or two enjoyable turns round the small ballroom floor before it became crowded. I often attended evening service at the Felixstowe Methodist Church before indulging in three or four hours of hard dancing. By leaving during the singing of the last hymn, I could catch the 7.30 bus from Felixstowe and thence cross the water by the connecting boat, all in good time for the band's first number of the evening.

Mostly, the music was provided by suitably talented RAF men. The "good" dancers knew each other and had a great time. I have recently had the good fortune to meet up with one of my special partners and when we have occasion to speak to each other on the 'phone, he introduces himself as "Fred" calling "Ginger"!

The social life at Bawdsey was quite wonderful and the spirit of camaraderie unique in my experience. How I wish I had kept a diary. "Dates" both on an individual level and in groups abounded. I had a glorious time. Most of the many lads I "walked out" with tended to want serious affairs, while I was very much the little "goody-goody", mean with my favours on the whole. As soon as the lads became intense, I usually dealt out the "elbow". I certainly cannot remember the names of all those I became involved with, so I will content myself in this chapter with a couple of comical rather than romantic stories. The more serious affairs I'll get to later.

In addition to the RAF personnel and soldiers from the nearby ack-ack batteries, members of the RAF Regiment attended the dances. A certain RAF Regiment sergeant found favour with me at one time. His attraction was simply that he "danced divinely", but on one occasion I was persuaded to accept an invitation to go walking with him.

Besides guarding the camp, the RAF Regiment's duties involved putting the airmen through an assault course at fairly frequent intervals. No doubt this was very necessary considering the sedentary nature of the work undertaken by the technical "bods". My RAF Regiment sergeant decided that our walk should, in part, cover the area used for the assault course. When we came to a small stream he explained, with some relish, that the puny radar men had to leap across the stream as part of their training. As we crossed, using a plank placed for the not so athletic, he enlarged on the stories of the trainees' lack of fitness; he had nothing but contempt for the technical men. Alas, I discovered that my companion's conversation was not up to the standard of his dancing and that he was something of a bore.

When we reached the stream on the homeward walk, we found that some playful spirit had removed the plank, and had thrown it down on the far side of the water. My boastful friend found that he had to emulate the much-derided RAF trainees and leap the stream. Predictably, he was not up to the task and landed wet and embarrassed, about a foot from the bank. To make matters worse he then toppled backwards and ended up sitting in the water!

There were, of course, a great many airfields in East Anglia. The American personnel of one such station, Martlesham, welcomed any interested WAAF to their dances and sent transport to convey us. I took up the offer on a few occasions, the attraction, apart from the dancing, being the delicious food on offer. In wartime Britain there were many food restrictions, none of which applied to the American services. For example, the manufacture of ice cream was not permitted for home consumption, but there were always gallons of the stuff to be had at Martlesham.

Another novelty at Martlesham was the presence of aircraft. At Bawdsey, the only aircraft we saw were flying overhead or blips on the screen. It was exciting to watch operational planes returning to land one after another. The men of the station always knew exactly how many planes had flown out and how many were due to return; they interrupted their dancing from time to time to dash out and ask colleagues how many were back, or if an overdue plane had shown up.

One day at Martlesham, a charming young officer took me out onto the airfield to show me the aircraft he flew. Together we clambered onto the wing to get a view of the cockpit of the Thunderbolt. For one who worked on an aircraft-less radar station it was exciting stuff, and the most interesting event of the evening. The episode did however cause a little embarrassment the next day.

On the few occasions when, because of adverse weather conditions, the Bawdsey screens were not busy, the people on watch could, and did, carry on conversations over the intercom. Three members of the watch were linked by the intercom system, and with no operational information to pass on, they invariably chattered. Two other people wore headsets enabling them to listen, but not to speak. One was listening for the purpose of recording information, and one headset was worn by a person at the CHL site, ready to alert their watch of any activity approaching the area. The two unfortunate earphone wearers had to listen to the conversation of the other three, no matter how inane the nattering might be. Of course, they could not remove their headsets in case a plane entered the area and operations began.

On the day after the Martlesham dance, I happened to be one of the three with a headset and a mouthpiece, when the conversation went something like this.

"Did you go to Martlesham last night, Gwen?"

"Yes."

"Have a good time?"

"The dancing was nothing special. The best bit was when an officer took me on to the airfield and showed me his Thunderbolt."

The remark was made in all innocence and did not provoke any special comment from the listeners in the CH operations room, but the entrapped listener in the CHL operations room quite understandably fell about, and thought my remark worth recording in the station magazine. I was very naïve. I wish I still had a copy of the *Bawdsey Star* which asks "Who was the WAAF who went to Martlesham and was shown an American officer's thunderbolt?"

If Bawdsey Manor became a luxury hotel, clients would pay the earth to stay there. It is wonderfully placed. Beach and sea on one side, river and boating just as close and the countryside stretching away from the other boundaries. We realised how lucky we were to be spending our service years in such an idyllic spot. As the war progressed and the fear of invasion receded, the amenities were extended to include sea bathing. A stretch of beach was de-mined and the barricades removed. We were permitted to wear civilian beach clothes and to bathe from the private beach — the Manor was a mere 50 yards from the water's edge. What could be more convenient and enjoyable?

We often spent off-duty time sunbathing on the shingle and bathed almost daily in the summer. Today, I would be nervous that one or two mines had been overlooked, but then, I suppose it was in 1945, we just had a wonderful time on our private beach.

Not content with daylight bathing, a few illegal midnight bathing parties were arranged — tremendous fun, but we usually forgot how sound travels in still night air. Our shrieks and screams could, I was told, be heard clearly in the Manor.

Another amenity we used to the full was the flat roof space between the turrets of both the Red and the White towers. On hot summer days, our "biscuits" would be hauled onto the roof and post night-watch sleeping enjoyed in the open air.

CHAPTER
TWENTY-THREE

John

For some months before "D-day" most of the south and east coast was declared a special area and unauthorised travel within the area forbidden. As a result, no leave could be taken. Hitherto, one seven-day leave had been permitted every three months, and eagerly anticipated home visits had taken place. The eight months without leave was a real hardship.

Shortly before the travel restrictions were imposed, a lad I had corresponded with for some time returned to the UK. I really did not know him well; we had exchanged only one or two "Good mornings" at the office where we both worked before joining up. His mother had also worked in the same office, and after John joined the army, at her request, I started writing to him from time to time. A rather lethargic correspondence continued from 1940 to 1944. We really knew little of one another and both found the obligation to write rather a chore.

John was a gun-site radar operator in Malta all through the siege years, enduring terrible conditions and non-stop bombardment by both the Germans and

Italians. (Per square mile, Malta was the most heavily bombed area of the war.)

In time the action moved away from Malta; the pressure was removed from the George Cross Island by our troops' successes in North Africa. After two years of bombing, hunger and hardship, John found peaceful Malta boring and in his own words he "volunteered for everything".

He was accepted for SAS training and posted to North Africa. There he was involved in a parachuting accident, when the American plane carrying the trainees allowed them to jump while over a mountainside. There was not sufficient height and some of the men were killed. John was fortunate, he only broke his nose and was soon able to resume training.

Shortly after completing his SAS training, one of the other assignments he had volunteered for came up. He was invited to appear before a commission board and he accepted the invitation.

All this time John's letters were censored and during the eight months around D-day — and mine were censored too. Censorship very much inhibits letter writers, especially when the officers who perform the task are your day-by-day companions. Certainly, many of the more interesting events of our lives could not be related, and so it is perhaps not surprising that after three or four years of such correspondence, we were still only casual acquaintances.

In February 1944, I was amazed to receive a phone call from John, who was, I thought, in North Africa.

He had returned to the UK to commence his officer training course. Suddenly our relationship began to flourish.

John had always been a good-looking young man, over six feet tall, bronzed and blue-eyed, but now the boy who left the office in 1940 had developed into a rugged and mature man — all that my Hollywood-inspired expectations could desire. Having spent much time at Bawdsey warding off the attentions of amorous young men, I now found myself spending a great deal of time with someone who did interest me very much, and who appeared to enjoy being with me.

When John phoned me with the news that he expected to spend several months in the UK, he asked if I could get leave to spend some time in Bournemouth with him. It must have been just before the travel restrictions because I have a letter from John written on 28th February '44, in which he suggests that while on leave, we might spend an evening at a Dinner Dance at the Swiss Restaurant in Bournemouth.

By 4th March John was writing in very affectionate terms, and referring to time spent together in Bournemouth while I was on a 48-hour leave pass. We had travelled back as far as London together and John had seen me on to my train at Liverpool Street, before continuing to the Royal Military Academy at Woolwich.

I received the following telegram from John on 7th March.

SENT LETTER PROBABLY DELAYED —
ARRIVE IPSWICH 1500 THURSDAY — TELL
NOBODY I AM COMING — LOVE JOHN
READING.

All very dramatic and exciting. As instructed, I told no
one of our tryst, but later found that John's mother
knew all about it, in fact I suspect that she may have
suggested the venture. No doubt John felt that if my
mother had known, she would have felt anxious about
the two nights we were proposing to spend
un-chaperoned under the same roof.

I obtained another pass, and still have the hotel
receipt (John has removed the part showing amounts)
for the nights of 9th and 10th March 1944, spent at the
Copdock Hotel. We occupied rooms 6 and 10 and had
a glorious two days. Not exactly a case of "Room Five
Hundred and Four" but it all fitted in beautifully with
my Hollywood-inspired expectations.

By 14th March, John had been posted to Wrotham
in Kent for his Pre-OCTU course. He asks if I
"successfully met Dorothy etc", which suggests to me
that I told my mother that I was spending my leave
with Dorothy. I would be surprised if I deceived my
mother, but perhaps it was kind to do so since, had she
rung while I was away, alarm and despondency could
have resulted. John seems to have been at the start of a
period of intense training, with not a minute to
breathe. He also mentions that London is out of
bounds to the Cadets. Anyone attempting to get to
London would be RTU'd (returned to unit)
immediately.

Dorothy was posted away from Bawdsey on the 18th of April and from that day leave was restricted. To the best of my recollection, we were not allowed to travel to coastal areas. However, by the 18th of April John's OCTU had been moved to Camberley which was outside the restricted area, and on the 25th I travelled south to spend an afternoon with him.

His letters, which continued to come thick and fast, were warm and affectionate. A week before my Camberley visit he wrote of my "project being delightful" (the visit of the 25th), but seemed to think that there were risks involved. His course had only two weeks to run and then maybe we could visit Copdock again.

I have clear recollection of the Camberley visit because suddenly there seemed to be a change in John. When we said goodbye on Camberley station, I received just a "brotherly" kiss. I returned to Bawdsey, beginning to suspect that perhaps Hollywood had got it all wrong. Maybe one did not fall in love as portrayed on the silver screen; perhaps one had to settle for less than perfection.

The next missive received from John was a rather "down" one in which he said he was going to drop an "awful brick". The brick was that he regarded our friendship as "purely platonic". Years later he told me that they had just been told that they were to complete their officer training in India, and from there would be bound for Burma. This was depressing news because Burma was considered the most hazardous war zone, and in John's own words "the few who came back

159

would most likely be maimed". He felt he had no right to ask me to wait for him. He did not tell me this at the time, and I came to the conclusion that I had read more into his intentions than was meant.

Despite this apparent change of heart on John's part, he wired me on 9th May thus:

UNABLE TO GET THROUGH ON THE PHONE BEFORE GOING ON EMBARK-ATION LEAVE SATURDAY FOR TWO WEEKS CANNOT TRAVEL THROUGH LONDON WRITE TO BOURNEMOUTH ANY CHANCE OF LEAVE LOVE JOHN.

It seems I managed to get an SOP (sleeping-out pass) despite Bournemouth being an out-of-bounds zone. No doubt having a friend on embarkation leave was reason enough for a special concession to be made. The letter posted on 19th May was cheerful and we had it seems a pleasant time together.

Letters continued to arrive every few days. It seems John did not embark with the first batch of men but was definitely in line for the next. He was in Bournemouth on more leave on 18th June.

Speaking now from memory I was by this time convinced that John did not care for me as I cared for him. It seemed to me that I was now the pursuer, which I perhaps deserved to be, after so often being the pursued. John's numerous letters were cool, and understandably, I was it seems, returning coolish replies. He speaks of not hearing from me for some days, and what brick has he dropped now? I suppose I wanted to be asked to make some commitment, but John continued to write about his dog, his relations, my relations and other dull subjects.

I received a rather frantic letter card from his mother, posted on 26th June. John was anxious about me because he did not know where he stood with me!

I felt I had done everything I could to promote the affair, dashing about the country on special concession passes only to be rewarded with bread and butter letters about "bricks" and "platonic friendships". I remember the emotional upheaval so well. Then I received another very "down" letter from John in which he described himself as a "bore", and complained that all his friends were "fixed up" while he was still taking Victor (his spaniel) out.

I must have replied with a reassuring letter because on the 30th of June I received another wire:

YOUR LETTER OF TUESDAY RECEIVED MANY THANKS AM JUST RETURNING LOVE JOHN.

I did manage to see him again before he embarked. He refers to spending $7^{1}/_{2}$ together in London on the 10th of July. In the last letter he wrote before leaving the UK (13th July), he asks "who is the considerate corporal who will meet you whichever train you travel back on?" I now find myself wondering the same thing. A corporal did figure largely in my life later on, but was he already dancing attendance? I do not remember.

Even so, John ends his letter thus:

"I feel that your visit was a very apt conclusion to my stay in England, in fact you, my dear, have made things so much brighter than they would have otherwise been."

Back at Bawdsey work and play continued. The play became a little more abandoned. Most of my companions were becoming married, engaged or at least "spoken for". After playing hard to get for ages, I was now the recipient of a "turn down", and very disappointed by John's apparent indifference. We continued to correspond, but our letters were as uninspired as ever. Clearly this was not the great romance but life had to go on.

CHAPTER
TWENTY-FOUR

Enter the V1s and V2s

Work, of course, continued, but to some extent the pattern was changing. In addition to masses of activity by our own aircraft and some intervention by German planes, the V1 menace had moved to the East Coast. Every day, numbers of these nasty little pilot-less aircraft zoomed into our area. Operationally they were very distinctive, we did not need Stanmore to identify these tracks. Flying low and in a dead straight line, they moved much faster than any known plane. Fortunately, the local gunners became expert at exploding them and few got past the coastline. They were far less frightening than conventional aircraft.

We were no longer forced to leave our beds when the air raid warning sounded. The fact that the V1 was over a legitimate target was of no consequence, because we all knew that it would fly on until its fuel ran out, or the ack-ack boys got it. As long as the fiery tail could be seen speeding across the sky, we knew we were quite safe. For the most part the girls half sat up in bed, leaning on an elbow to watch the show; when the gunners scored a direct hit and the whole thing blew up in mid-air it was quite spectacular.

When the V2 rockets came along, special equipment was installed in the CH block. Known as "Oswald", the screen showed a faint but distinctive threadlike track when a V2 scorched through the stratosphere. The operator then yelled "Big Ben at Bawdsey" down the line to the Filter room. We understood that a four-minute warning could have been given to the people of London. The authorities decided not to give an alarm and perhaps they were right, since the entire London population would have been disrupted and sent scurrying to the shelters, for an explosion which was only going to affect one area, albeit a tremendous and devastating explosion.

The screen of Oswald had to be watched very intently. The tracks were so small and appeared so briefly, that they could be missed altogether if the operator blinked. The watcher had to be changed every fifteen minutes, whereas the ordinary operational screen could be observed for an hour.

A few minutes after the "Big Ben at Bawdsey" call, Stanmore sent instructions to "change Oswald"; this was our cue to remove the film which ran within Oswald and develop it. Stanmore staggered the times for changing Oswald, so that no two stations would be off the air at the same time.

The supervisors were trained to analyse the filmed trace, and from the information gathered by a group of stations, the location of the launching pads could be ascertained. Members of the watch were required to develop the films in an improvised dark room, a shed in the CH block compound. It was more than a little eerie walking through the pitch-blackness of the night and then, by the light of a tiny red bulb, developing the precious film. To speed up the drying operation the film was wound round a frame and spun over an electric heater. I recall an occasion when I neglected to secure a frame properly; as soon as the spinning operation started, the whole thing fell onto the heater with disastrous results.

I think it was about this time that a bombing raid on the station caused a fatality. For the most part attacks on the station had caused little damage. On this occasion, an airman died when his billet was hit; he had been sitting up in bed and was said to have been decapitated. Had he been lying down, in all probability he would have survived. We all felt his death keenly, especially as he had been engaged to one of the airwomen.

Another tragedy, which upset us all very greatly, occurred when a WAAF cook tripped and fell while she was carrying a bucket of caustic soda. She literally fell into a pool of caustic soda and was terribly burned. She died some weeks later in Ipswich hospital.

CHAPTER
TWENTY-FIVE

After John

On the social front, there was another exchange of letters which had continued in a leisurely way. Since Cranwell days, Donald, who had charmed me so much with his piano playing, had kept in touch by letter. Quite soon after John left for India, Donald wrote informing me that he was to be posted to Market Harborough, and as he would be quite near to London, could we arrange to meet? We spent several 48-hour passes together in London, always enjoying the luxury of good hotels and wallowing in our shared enthusiasm for the music of Chopin. Donald, blond and round faced, was not as handsome as John, nor quite as tall, but he was attentive and sentimental and he made one feel very special. He was a lovely restful person to be with.

Where John had shown so much diffidence, Donald swept me off my feet. On 21st March 1945 he proposed marriage and I accepted. At the time it seemed right; perhaps the fact that most of my friends were engaged, either officially or unofficially, or married, influenced me. So many of my boyfriends had popped the question — except the one I had singled out as fitting the bill. It was comfortable to feel that I belonged to someone as dear as Donald. I told my family and friends, and in my next letter to John I told him the news.

At the same time an announcement was placed in the *Bournemouth Daily Echo*. On seeing this, John's mother wrote post-haste to tell John, and it so happened that her letter arrived before mine. The resulting letter that John wrote to me, by its very formality, gave me for the first time, an inkling that he had indeed thought of me as more than a "platonic friend". I'll quote the letter in full:

"At dinner tonight I had a letter from Mother. She told me about you becoming engaged and forthcoming marriage. I thought I ought to write straight away and congratulate you on these speedy events. You may be sure I was surprised since you had mentioned nothing of this to me before. However, I must take this opportunity of proffering my congratulations and wish you and your future husband all happiness.

May I just for the last time thank you most sincerely for the constant letters that have come from you through the post for the last four years, and last but by no means least for the very pleasant time I had in England in your company last year.

Please remember me to your Mother, Peggy, Bill and Robbie."

No more letters came from John, confirming the impression I now received that he had perhaps thought of me as more than an acquaintance. His mother, who had always kept in touch, wrote no more, suggesting to me that she too had thought that there had been some sort of understanding between us. Obviously, I had hurt them both.

But back to Donald. After one or two further happy meetings and a number of letters, Donald and I planned to spend 48 hours together starting on 8th May 1945. We had booked rooms in Felixstowe and I expected a pleasant two days making vague plans for the future; but Donald arrived full of news and immediate plans. He was to be posted overseas in two weeks' time and wanted us to be married before he left. That day we were to go to Ipswich, buy the ring, arrange a special licence, draft an announcement for the *Telegraph* and make detailed plans for the event.

This is a scene I remember with great clarity. Donald was unpacking his case in the small boarding house and excitedly outlining his plans. Quite suddenly, I knew I could not marry him. While marriage had been an airy-fairy prospect, planned for an unknown date in the future, it was a nice comfortable state of affairs; but when the event was timed for a few days hence, I was full of doubts. At the time I had not received John's letter revealing that perhaps our friendship did matter to him, so that was not an influencing factor. I can only say very lamely, that Donald was just too "nice".

It was one of those moments which changed the

whole of two lives — mine and Donald's. Would it have been better if I had acted differently? I shall never know. In retrospect, my behaviour seems unbelievably callous and cruel.

I told Donald that I could not go through with his plans and that the engagement was off. The poor boy packed his bags and caught the next train to London, en route for his home in Lancashire. It was VE day. I still feel a great wave of guilt when I think of Donald travelling through London where the celebrations were so tremendous, while he was so very unhappy. It was an appallingly badly chosen day to make a fellow human being desperately miserable.

For my part I returned to Bawdsey on the next bus, crossed the ferry and immediately walked into the corporal in charge of "C" watch, another John. He was surprised to see me back; the whole watch knew that I had set off to spend two days with my fiancé. I had to give an explanation and so told John briefly the happenings of the day.

I had the grace to be upset. We walked along the beach together and finally stretched out on the shingles and talked for a long time. I did not deserve the kindness he showed me.

Looking back, I think perhaps John C and I had been aware of each other for some time. I swear that my conscious mind did not know how I felt about him before that day; nor did I know that he cared for me when I sent Donald on his way. My subconscious must have been influencing my actions greatly at that time.

John C looked after me for the rest of the day. I

remember walking to tea together, appreciating his support and becoming less tearful.

I am ashamed to say that I ended up enjoying the rest of VE day with my colleagues. Not only was it fantastic to be celebrating the end of the war, but I celebrated with the person who was to become my soul-mate, and who I believe to be the great love of my life.

There was, of course, a party to end all parties that night. Sunday evening dances paled into insignificance. The celebrations went on nearly all night and it was the most joyful occasion imaginable. For once the NAAFI coffee was replaced by "scrumpy", and very potent stuff it was too, and yet I have no recollection of drunkenness. The celebrations were as near to pure joy as one could get.

The next few weeks were perhaps the most magical of my youth. Every free moment was spent with John C. Bawdsey provided an ideal setting in which to be young and in love. We were completely in tune.

Once again I became engaged and my poor mother began to be somewhat embarrassed by the frequency of my betrothals; also, I suspect, rather worried about me.

In about July 1945 John C. was posted to Thame in Oxfordshire. We then met frequently in London and continued to be very happy.

On one occasion we spent a weekend in Bournemouth with my mother and sister. My home circumstances were not nearly as grand as those enjoyed by John. His father was a dental surgeon, and he himself had been training to become a dental surgeon before his studies had been interrupted by the war. Our home in Bournemouth was not prepossessing and I was very aware of the wide difference in our backgrounds.

CHAPTER
TWENTY-SIX

No Longer At War

VJ day (August 8th) came along and of course was greeted with more celebrations. John C was not at Bawdsey, but it was a memorable occasion, the festivities again continuing until 4am and "scrumpy" provided once more. I have a clear recollection of the night ending with great lines of us conga-ing through the grounds, preceded by four or five dustbin-lid-beating celebrators.

The sheer joy of no longer being at war was beyond description. Today, when memories of the war years are revived by those who were part of them, we are inclined to give the impression that it was all tremendous fun, a great adventure and that we were having the time of our lives. It was all of that, but we forget to mention the traumas and deprivations of our unnatural living conditions, and how each one of us longed and lived for the day when life would be normal once more. Civvy Street was Utopia. Our eager desire was to sleep in homely beds, wear civilian clothes, go to work, earn a normal wage and be free from the unnatural discipline of service life. Equally importantly, one longed to know that the world was going forward again, that mass destruction was finished, and that the efforts of the people would be constructive from now on.

We had been fighting for freedom from tyranny, the aggression of dictators and a lot more besides. During the war I didn't meet a single pacifist; although I suppose there were some. All the people I knew were wholeheartedly behind the war effort. We believed in the cause for which we were fighting, believed that it was right and just. I thought it to be so then; I know it to have been so now. We had witnessed the disarmament and appeasement of the 30s, and we knew these two to be tragic follies. While one ruthless and determined aggressor remains, only strength deters.

With the war over, the whole atmosphere of service life changed. The urgency and common cause vanished overnight; now all our thoughts were centred on Civvy Street, and what we were going to make of our lives from that day on. We were going to make up for the time unstintingly given to the task of freeing the world from unspeakable tyranny. On-camp entertainment faded away, no-one spent free time on the station if they could possibly avoid doing so. Those who lived reasonably near seemed able to get endless sleeping-out passes.

The work of radar stations became academic. We had only our own aircraft on training and routine flights to plot and bureaucracy moved in where commonsense and urgency had ruled hitherto.

There was, for example, a great programme of misemployment. The effect was that many were engaged in work for which they had received no training, and which was rather less important than their original trade. Masses of redundant aircrew were posted to Bawdsey and they manned the watches. They were bright lads, but being recently relieved of their dangerous and nerve-racking trade, they considered radar just a fun job.

The radar operators were posted away to large aerodromes and headquarters, there to be employed as clerks.

Clearly, all service personnel could not be released *en masse*. The whole industrial structure of the nation had to be reorganised, and released men and women channelled into suitable employment. Employers who were still in business were obliged to take back their former employees; clearly they could not deal with the situation at the drop of a hat. The masses of temporary employees who had kept things going throughout the war now had to be eased back to their former roles as housewives or pensioners. In those days, few married women wanted or expected to work once peace returned.

A system of gradual release was evolved. Every serviceman and woman was given a rating calculated by reference to age and date of entry into the forces. Selected numbers from each trade were then released month by month. In this way there was a steady trickle of people returning to civilian life, and as far as I am aware the system worked well enough. Married girls were the exception; they were released straight away, presumably to make homes for their returning spouses.

If we longed for our return to civilian life during the war, now we desired it urgently and impatiently. We daily scanned the notice boards for our particular demob numbers to appear. To "get out" became everyone's great objective; the old spirit of camaraderie waned and almost died.

When my misemployment started in October 1945, I had to collect together the debris of my two and a half years at Bawdsey, bicycle, pillows, a whole lot of "civvies" and of course my official kit, load it on to the ferryboat and make my final trip across the Deben. My posting was to Fighter Command Headquarters in Uxbridge, where I was obliged to work out the rest of my time as an orderly room clerk. It could only be termed an anti-climax after the days of picking up and plotting masses of friendly and hostile aircraft, "doodlebugs" and rockets over the North Sea, but I had to make the best of it.

The living accommodation at Uxbridge was dreadful, or perhaps it was just that I had been spoiled at Bawdsey. The huts, which slept about a dozen girls, were said to have been condemned in 1932. I could believe this to be true. Heating was by means of an iron stove in the middle of the room; reasonable enough when used, but all too frequently the stove was out. We were so often on leave or otherwise engaged, that we never seemed able to establish a workable rota for firelighting. Throughout that very cold winter more often than not the hut was fireless. At weekends the hut was often unoccupied; those who lived in the London area spent every weekend at home. On many occasions I hitch-hiked quite alone to Bournemouth, returning by train on Sunday evening. I recall returning one Sunday evening to find the violets I had left on my locker completely sealed in a block of ice!

Fighter Command HQ was at the Hillingdon end of RAF Uxbridge and quite separate from the main base. We mostly entered by the Uxbridge gate, which meant quite a long walk through the camp and finally crossing a small stream by bridge to reach our end of the camp. A ghost was said to haunt the bridge, making the trek to the cheerless hut on dark winter nights quite stressful. I did not see the apparition, but dreaded crossing the bridge after dark or at dusk. It was not jolly.

The work was boringly routine, and every third or fourth night an all-night duty had to be performed in the dirty little post room. As duty clerk one had to await signals and direct them onwards to the duty officer, or whoever was concerned. Few signals came through, and so in theory the clerk could sleep most of the night, but the only horizontal surface in the room, apart from the floor, was the wooden table and the only bedding a grubby blanket. It was solitary, eerie and thoroughly unpleasant — so unlike the radar night watches of worthwhile activity, bustle and fun.

Social activity on the camp was almost nil, but I frequently met John C in London and our time together continued to be memorable and very happy.

As our release dates drew nearer, we began to make plans for the future. I met John's mother who lived in London, also his sister and her Group Captain husband. John's parents were divorced and I did not have an opportunity to meet his father who lived and worked in Bristol. John considered his home to be with his father and intended to complete his dentistry training and to become part of the family business.

One day, quite out of the blue, I received a letter from John C telling me that his father was refusing to finance his training unless he agreed to postpone marriage until the training was completed. Looking back on the matter, I can see his father's point of view, but at the time I saw it as a straight but difficult choice for John, between his training and me. I could not visualise our relationship continuing as it was for two years and living together was not an option in those days; I could not put my family through the shame of having a daughter involved in such an arrangement. I wrote to John telling him that our engagement must end. Did I expect him to forego his training? I really do not know. I received several letters of reasoned argument from him. I did not reply.

Wretched Hollywood told me that "true love" would not let any obstacle stand in its way. I took a very immature stand. Today one can opt for the best of all worlds. Then, the world viewed these things so very differently and at the time, sadly, I thought that I was right.

CHAPTER
TWENTY-SEVEN

The Big
Adventure Ends

In the early part of 1946, I was a very unhappy person. My family were not told the reason for the broken engagement, but they were aware of my miserable state and clearly worried about me. I spent a lot of my free time with an uncle and his family in Ruislip; they had been kept in the picture by my mother, and they very kindly did all they could to cheer me up.

My poor, worried mother came to stay in Ruislip for a week, which was a tremendous effort on her part. Although only about 55 years of age, she had not travelled more than a few miles from Bournemouth since she was a very young girl. I recall that when I met her at Waterloo station she was trembling visibly, so great was the undertaking to travel to London. Now a mother and a grandmother myself, I can understand her anxiety and how she felt compelled to put her own fears aside and do what she could for her lovesick daughter.

The humdrum existence at Uxbridge continued. As before, there were plenty of offers of male company.

Ex-flying crew were now being posted to Uxbridge to be misemployed as clerks, providing plenty of "talent". But I had returned to the frame of mind of the period before my spate of engagements, and turned all the invitations down.

The months slowly passed until June 1946 when at last, my group was posted to be demobbed in July. Wonderful news; now I could begin to plan for the future; I would be a civilian again. I had longed for this day for three and a half years.

On July 11th 1946, I found myself in Birmingham for the glorious demob procedure. Once again, I slept in a huge hut with 47 other girls . . . but who cared? This was our last night before freedom.

Getting out was a lot simpler than getting in; soon I was on my way to Bournemouth with a handful of clothing coupons and about £125 in gratuity and leave money.

Just to be at home was heaven. I shopped around for a few items of civvy clothes and began to view the world with cheerful anticipation once more.

My old job at the Bournemouth Gas & Water Company was waiting for me and on 31st August 1946 I started back, feeling that I was comparatively unchanged since the day in 1943 when the staff had sent me on my way with so many good wishes. But surely, so much fun, laughter, sadness and experience must have had some effect.

Halfway through my first morning back in the Costs office, a personal telephone call came through for me. I was tremendously embarrassed. In those days no one took telephone calls at work unless it was a matter of life and death. Who would do this to me, knowing that I would be hoping to make a good impression on my first day back? Wishing the ground would open up I picked up the receiver.

"Hello?"

"Hello, it's John (R) here. I've got two weeks' leave before I go back to Basra; will you have dinner with me tonight?"

My only thought was to keep the phone call short and reduce the embarrassment. I agreed and noted the time and place.

The phone call was another turning point. Had I not been so acutely embarrassed, the course of my personal history from then on might have been different . . .

So much has happened since the 31st August 1946.

CHAPTER
TWENTY-EIGHT

And Now — Year 2000

John and I were married on the 24th of April 1947 and we had 47½ happy years together. We were blessed with two lovely daughters and four delightful grandchildren.

I will not attempt to cover the years from the day in August 1946 when John came back into my life, as that would be a huge task. Suffice to say they were good years, with the usual mixture of joy and sadness, but far more joy than sadness.

Then on November 2nd 1994 John had a heart attack and suddenly I was alone.

After much thought and prayer I moved 450 miles to live near one of my daughters.

I now live in a small, brand-new house in Scotland and I am content. I still love the music of Chopin, I dance often, and have a new enthusiasm; I have filled my brand-new garden with roses.

ISIS publish a wide range of books in large print, from fiction to biography. Any suggestions for books you would like to see in large print or audio are always welcome. Please send to the Editorial Department at:

ISIS Publishing Ltd.
7 Centremead
Osney Mead
Oxford OX2 0ES
(01865) 250 333

A full list of titles is available free of charge from:
Ulverscroft Large Print Books

(UK)
The Green
Bradgate Road, Anstey
Leicester LE7 7FU
Tel: (0116) 236 4325

(Australia)
P.O Box 953
Crows Nest
NSW 1585
Tel: (02) 9436 2622

(USA)
1881 Ridge Road
P.O Box 1230, West Seneca,
N.Y. 14224-1230
Tel: (716) 674 4270

(Canada)
P.O Box 80038
Burlington
Ontario L7L 6B1
Tel: (905) 637 8734

(New Zealand)
P.O Box 456
Feilding
Tel: (06) 323 6828

Details of **ISIS** complete and unabridged audio books are also available from these offices. Alternatively, contact your local library for details of their collection of **ISIS** large print and unabridged audio books.